Endorsements

"Holly and Rachel are THE go-to resource for kids activities."

—**Debbie Clement**, creator of Rainbows within Reach

"Holly Homer and Rachel Miller are my go-to experts for play and learning activities."

—**Melissa Taylor**, author of *Pinterest Savvy*

"Holly and Rachel are two of the most creative people I know! I love their ideas for simple and easy kids activities with items you already have in your home."

—**Amy Locurto**, Living Locurto & I Heart Faces

"These activities will help your whole family have fun, bond and grow together."

—**Peg Fitzpatrick**, mom, writer and social media strategist

"Holly and Rachel provide innovative ideas every parent will love, and that keep kids engaged and learning!"

—**Tammy Kling**, bestselling author

"As an NFL mom of a preschooler, toddler and soon-to-be newborn, I love new creative activities that will keep kids entertained. Rachel and Holly are true geniuses of play."

—**Alissa Chandler**, NFL wife and mom

"As moms in the trenches, just like us, Holly and Rachel know what works with kids and what doesn't. If anyone should publish a book about kids and activities, it's these gals. They live the dream, and the messes, every day. They know what it takes and what it doesn't to keep kids busy and engaged. I'm excited about this book ... a book about kids activities that I am certain will reflect Holly and Rachel's own kids' activities 'street smarts'!"

—**Jenny Ingram**, Jenny on the Spot

"Finally. A book with more than 100 tried-and-true activities written by two of the best moms around. I'm sold!"

—**Laurie Turk**, TipJunkie.com

"Being a parent of a toddler, I've been a fan of the Kids Activities Blog for about a year now. It's a creative and fun resource for parents filled with ideas I would NEVER have come up with on my own. I'm looking forward to getting more ideas from this book!"

—**Dinah Wulf**, DIYinspired.com

"I am dying to see these 101 activities from Holly and Rachel! They have the funnest activities for kids that are so easy to do! This will definitely be a great resource!"

—**Jamie Reimer**, Hands On As We Grow

"I am always amazed and inspired by the number and diversity of their fabulous, child-focused projects! This book is an amazing go-to resource for any parent or caregiver."

—**Maggy Woodley**, author and blogger, Red Ted Art

From Holly
To Greg and my boys—Ryan, Reid & Rhett—who dependably never turn down a game.

From Rachel
To my mom—the woman who taught me to play—and to my kids, Lena, Ezra, Anya, Kora, Jonah & Noah, who keep fun alive in our home.

PAGE STREET
PUBLISHING CO.

First published in 2014 by
Page Street Publishing Co.
27 Congress Street, Suite 103
Salem, MA 01970
www.pagestreetpublishing.com

Distributed by Macmillan; sales in Canada by The Canadian Manda Group; distribution in Canada by The Jaguar Book Group.

17 16 15 14   4 5

ISBN13: 978-1-62414-057-0
ISBN10: 1-62414-057-2

Library of Congress Control Number: 2013920247

Cover and book design by Page Street Publishing
Photography by Tamara Lee-Sang

Printed and bound in China

Page Street is proud to be a member of 1% for the Planet. Members donate one percent of their sales to one or more of the over 1,500 environmental and sustainability charities across the globe who participate in this program.

101 kids activities

THAT ARE THE BESTEST, FUNNEST EVER!

THE ENTERTAINMENT SOLUTION FOR PARENTS, RELATIVES & BABYSITTERS!

Holly Homer & Rachel Miller

OF KIDSACTIVITIESBLOG.COM

PREFACE

The thing about kids is they grow up. They start out inquisitive, adventurous and wildly participatory. They find thrill in activities, silly games and simple crafts. Somewhere along the way a governor gets placed that says that inquiry can only be serious, adventures should be within a specific path and participation needs a leader.

Why is play constrained?

Why do adults look both ways before joining in?

Why isn't play the first thing on the family calendar?

Modern life has filled our schedules with things that we have to do. Modern life has filled our schedules with things our kids have to do. Modern life has held us captive indoors.

We *want* to play.

We *long* for time together.

We *seek* fun.

The good news is that play is waiting on us. It sits quietly giggling at the dining room table, under the bed, behind the curtains, in the kitchen junk drawer, in the trunk of the car, between the couch cushions and peeking through the door to the backyard.

Play doesn't mind if you stop by for just a moment. It is fine with being added to the situation at the last minute. It loves occupying those little moments between the scheduled ones and then sneaking into the rest of the day.

Play can take an ordinary day and make it a favorite day. It doesn't require equipment, money or planning. It can fill a moment. It can fill a day. And when intentionally sought out, it can fill a life.

We want to value time over toys. We want our kids to keep play close as they grow and weave it into their future. We want them to remember the times we played *together*.

Our fondest memories of childhood are those filled with play. Our bedrooms weren't filled with toys, they were chock-full of possibilities. Our play wasn't fancy or structured, it followed us around like an imaginary friend.

There were homemade wooden blocks in the living room and a rag doll on the bed. There were woods to explore and sketches of tree house plans waiting to be built. There were fireflies in a jar on the bedside table and a mysterious cocoon taped upright to the bookshelf. We had collections of rocks and a stack of home-made games created with items from the kitchen junk drawer. There was a garden outside that attracted sneaky rabbits and a swing whose arc was never-ending. There were diaries that held novels in progress and frozen containers of yogurt to eat on the back porch. There were distant travels on a magical throw rug and craft projects that required broken crayons and scraps of yarn. There were orchards that smelled like cider and snow that was shoveled into games of fox and hound. Stairs doubled as slides and bicycles rode faster than the wind. There were books to read and reread and blanket tents large enough for a revival. There were plays to write, act and direct with an audience of stuffed animals and card games that ended in playful boasts. There were endless trees to climb and imaginary friends to visit.

We hope that this book inspires you to find play in big and small moments every day. We hope it is an imagination boost that launches childhood memories beyond these pages.

We believe that you don't need the latest gadgets or an elaborate plan to engage children. Play meets everyone right where they are with what they have in their hand.

Sure, play is fun, but children will learn life skills that will stay with them forever. Finding joy, acting with diligence, teamwork, gratitude, mindfulness of others, patience, compassion, sportsmanship and respect are all play companions.

Play is family glue.

Let's play!

Holly & Rachel

Unless otherwise specified, each of these activities may be enjoyed by one or more participants. Often, our activities include optional modifications to take the age of the kid(s) into greater consideration. The suggested modifications for younger kids are more suitable for ages one to three; those for older kids are more suitable for ages four to ten. And of course, many of these activities are truly for "kids of all ages," so feel free to join in the fun!

Contents

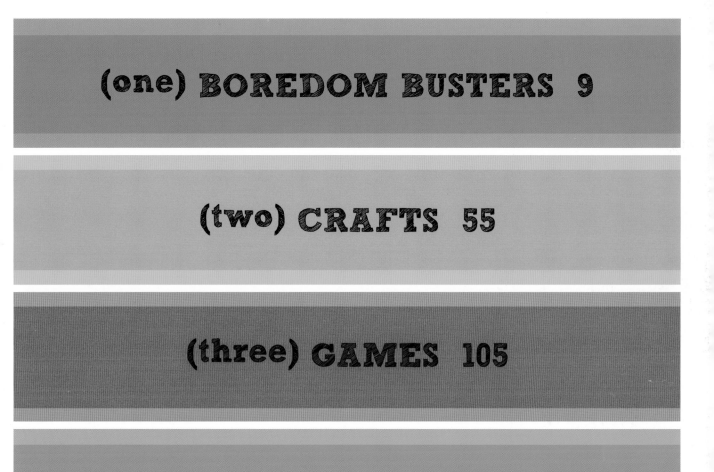

(one)

BOREDOM BUSTERS

Boredom is the garden in which play grows. It is a motivation
for action and a blank slate for creativity.

Holly's Chapter Pick: I think the Wooden Block Townhouses (page 53)
are delightful. There are a million ways to play with them and when not
in use they double as a precious room decoration.

Rachel's Chapter Pick: Building Paper Cup Castles (page 27) is one
of our kids' favorite things to do. Whenever I want/need the kids
to be engaged, it's time to bring out the stack of cups.
Your kids will love this activity!

Baggie Maze

Mazes are an adventure on paper. A single pencil line journeys into the unknown. There is a sense of wonder at each crossroad of the possibility of reaching the goal.

Creating a baggie maze is a fun craft that is also great entertainment on the go. It is something that can be dropped into a purse or bag to be used as a quiet-time game.

- -

Materials
(to make one double-sided maze)

+ SCISSORS
+ CARDBOARD—UPCYCLED FROM A CEREAL BOX OR OTHER RESCUED RECYCLABLE
+ RESEALABLE PLASTIC SANDWICH BAG
+ 4 OR 5 DRINKING STRAWS
+ GLUE DOTS OR TAPE
+ SMALL MARBLE OR OTHER OBJECT

TIP
Social scientists claim that doing mazes helps build brain connections and develop problem-solving skills.

Cut the cardboard into a square that snuggly fits into the sandwich bag. Clip one of the corners for a "start" and cut a quarter-size (2.5 cm-diameter) circle on another corner for the goal. Snip the straws into smaller pieces and use the glue dots to glue them on the cardboard, creating a maze path. (We used glue dots so we didn't need to wait for glue to dry.) You can also use tape.

The interior of the bag will create "sides" to the maze so the exterior of the cardboard square does not have to be outlined with straws. Place the marble in the maze, seal the bag and, holding the bag flat, tilt it to guide the marble through the maze.

Modifications for Younger Kids
For younger children, monitor them and either glue or tape the top of the bag closed. Also, creating an easier maze will result in less frustration for your child.

Modifications for Older Kids
Have older kids create a double-sided maze. They can then solve both sides of their baggie maze.

Bird Zip Line

Riding a zip line feels like you are flying. Spread your arms out wide and feel the wind on your face while you glide to the bottom. This craft builds a bird that will fly just like you can, zip line style! Create a string track and add a little kid power combined with gravity.

Materials
(to make one bird/zip line)

+ SHEET OF PAPER—CARDSTOCK IS BEST
+ PENCIL
+ SCISSORS
+ MARKERS/CRAYONS
+ TAPE
+ DRINKING STRAW
+ BALL OF YARN

To make the bird: Fold a piece of paper in half lengthwise and trace out the profile of a flying bird on one half with the fold at the top. Cut along the pencil lines. Use markers to decorate the bird. Open the bird and tape a straw along the inside fold.

To make the zip line: Stretch the yarn between two secure anchor spots where string can be attached. It should be at a height that kids can easily reach. Thread a bird onto each string before tying both ends of it to the anchor spots.

Kids can "throw" the birds down the yarn to make them fly. Multiple zip lines can be set up next to each other for bird races.

Modifications for Younger Kids
Placing the string at kid-size shoulder level will have younger participants running up and down the yarn, holding the bird.

Modifications for Older Kids
Have older kids design a bird that is bottom-heavy and then split the underside of the straw so that the bird can be unattached and reattached from the string without untying the ends. Then challenge older kids to create a zip line course for their bird to fly.

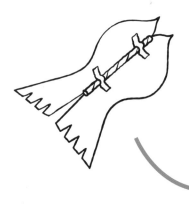

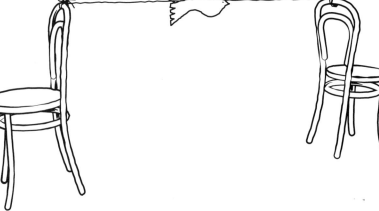

Dry-Erase Doodles

My favorite thing to draw as a child was a sunrise. After a visit to the mountains, I modified my regular pattern to include pointy snowcapped mountains in the background behind the sun. It was years later when someone mentioned to me that there was no possible way for the sun to rise in front of the mountains! It was my own artistic license.

This activity box is a really easy travel or rainy-day activity. There are suggested templates to place in a CD case and transform into an artistic masterpiece with dry-erase markers, but the possibilities are endless.

Materials

+ EMPTY CLEAR CD CASE
+ A VARIETY OF PAPER PAGES, PHOTOS, MAPS, ETC.
+ SCISSORS
+ DRY-ERASE MARKERS

TIP

Sneak a few unexpected templates in the box when no one is looking, for a fun surprise.

Create a Doodle Board Background

The inside of a CD case is 5½ x 4¾ inches (14 x 12 cm). Create a background for doodling by cutting different templates to size from your paper collection and inserting them into the case.

IDEAS FOR BACKGROUNDS

• **Kid photo**—Doodle to add character and fun!

• **Hangman gallows**—Start a game of Hangman by drawing the gallows template. Kids can play over and over.

• **Kid-created maze**—Give kids properly sized paper to draw a maze and then place the maze in another box for someone else to solve.

• **Open sky**—Add a piece of light blue paper to the box for clouds, planes and birds to be doodled.

• **Black box**—Insert a plain piece of paper with just a black box drawn in the middle. Have kids create whatever they can imagine around the box.

The good news is that a CD case will hold multiple templates and they can be kept and stored in the case.

Modifications for Younger Kids

Create a series of letter and number cards that kids can trace.

Modifications for Older Kids

Have older children design the backgrounds of their box within a theme that they love. Try a fashion series of color swatches, dress forms and blank bodies to accessorize.

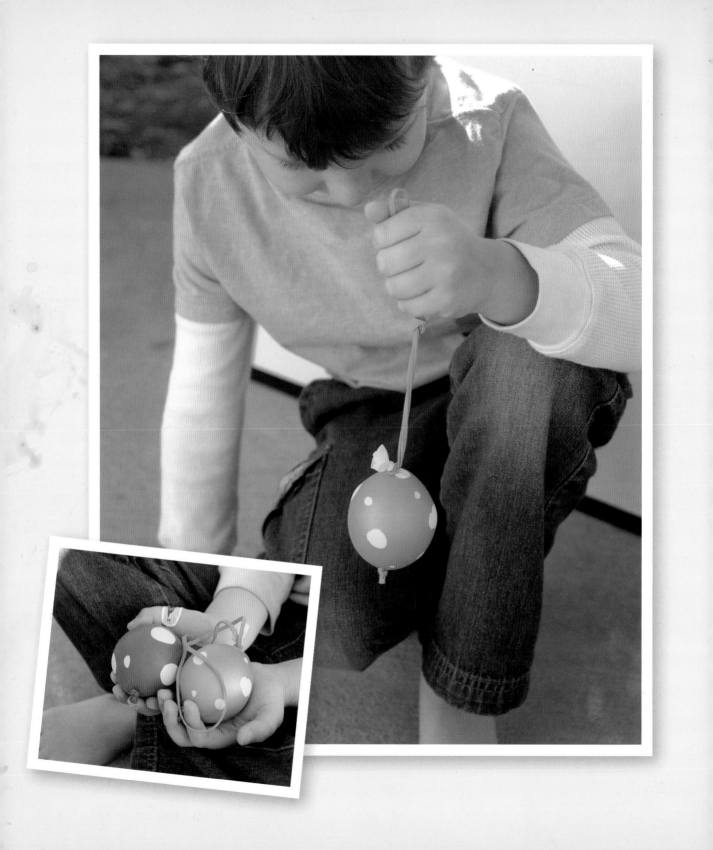

Bouncing Balloons

Yo-yos go down and then defy gravity with an unexpected ascent. The rhythmic drop and return require skill both physically and mentally. Making a yo-yo follow your lead and continue its momentum is a challenge for anyone, regardless of age.

While you can't do all the traditional yo-yo tricks with this homemade version, it is a fun way to practice eye-hand coordination. It is created from balloons, play dough and rubber bands, allowing it to mimic the yo-yo action, which is much easier to control.

Materials

+ Colorful balloons
+ Play dough (see page 19), sand or flour
+ Scissors
+ Large rubber band (or multiple bands if small)
+ Masking tape

TIP

Play dough, sand or flour in a balloon mimics the adult "stress ball" and can be a source of calming sensation to kids.

Fill the balloon with the play dough. If you don't have play dough you can use flour or sand. Then, tie the balloon shut.

Cut some small holes into a second balloon. Carefully stretch the second balloon over the play dough–filled balloon, allowing the color of the lower balloon to peek through the top layer holes.

Tie the rubber band around the knot in the balloon. If your rubber band is not long enough, make a "string" of bands by tying them to each other.

To play, draw an X on the floor with tape and use it as a target. Try to bounce the yo-yo on the object to see how many times you can bounce it.

Modifications for Younger Kids

Skip the rubber bands and game. Let the kids squish the filled yo-yo ball.

Modifications for Older Kids

Set up a series of numbered X's on the floor in a random pattern and instruct the child to work through the numbers in sequence. Each time an incorrect number is hit, the game starts over at the number one.

DIY
Straw Building Set

We think of this activity as straw doodling, because an ordinary straw can be transformed by the insertion of a pipe cleaner. This simple alteration can create a building set to be used over and over in different and magnificent ways.

Materials

+ Box (or 3) of flexible drinking straws
+ Scissors
+ Pipe cleaners (optional)
+ Tape

To put your straws together, pinch one end of a straw and stuff it into the connecting straw. Using the angles of the flexible straws, repeat until you have the desired shape, cutting the straws, if needed. If it is too difficult for your children to stuff the straws together, thread the pipe cleaners through the straws to use as connectors.

Kids can create all sorts of 3-D shapes, buildings and art sculptures by manipulating the straws. In addition to being stuffed together, straw pieces can be attached to each other by twisting the end of the pipe cleaners run through them. Shapes created by straws can be attached to each other with a simple piece of tape for even more possibilities. Creations can be as large as the amount of materials you might have!

Modifications for Younger Kids

For younger participants, use pipe cleaners and straws to create an endless loop for them to play with so they don't have to attach pipe cleaner ends together. They will enjoy bending and shaping their circle into new shapes.

Modifications for Older Kids

Have older kids test out several sizes of straws before creating the full set. Let them test build and determine what size materials they want for their building project and then create the set within those parameters.

Edible Play Dough

Playing with play dough is one of our favorite activities. With this activity, I've figured out a way to get my kids to enjoy play dough and make our dinner at the same time! The secret is homemade pasta noodles. Egg-based pasta dough is perfect for molding and can be colored red or green with beet or spinach juice. The kids play while the dough is transformed into dinner.

Materials
(to make 3½ cups [about 400 g] play dough)

+ LARGE MIXING BOWL
+ STRONG WOODEN OR METAL SPOON
+ 3 CUPS (375 G) ALL-PURPOSE FLOUR
+ ½ TEASPOON (3 G) SALT
+ 1 EGG
+ ¼ CUP (60 G) SOUR CREAM
+ ⅓ CUP (80 ML) MILK (SEE TIP)
+ 2 TO 3 TABLESPOONS (30 TO 45 ML) OLIVE OIL
+ BEET OR SPINACH JUICE TO DYE THE DOUGH (OPTIONAL; SEE TIP)

TIP
The amount of juice depends on how dark you want your noodles to be. We add roughly 2 tablespoons (30 ml) of juice dye to a cup of dough, but if your kids enjoy the taste of spinach you can add even more! You can replace the milk with the vegetable juice if you prefer.

To make the dough: In a bowl, mix all the dry ingredients together well with your hands or a strong wooden or metal spoon. Add the egg, sour cream, milk and oil. Add the juice, if using. The dough will be incredibly stiff. Cover it and put it in the fridge for a few hours. I usually make the dough in advance and store it in an airtight container in the refrigerator.

After the dough has "sat" for a few hours, it becomes more elastic and less stiff. Knead and play with the dough. The more your dough is played with, the better your noodles will become!

Form noodles by making dozens and dozens of "little worms." This is my kids' favorite part. If you enjoy a variety of noodle shapes, consider making small balls of dough and then flattening them. Those are tasty when they become dumplings. You can also roll out the dough into a sheet and cut the noodles into thin strips.

After your kids have had fun creating worms and a variety of noodle shapes, bring a pot of water to a boil. Add some sea salt and the noodles to the water and boil until they are fully cooked. It usually takes 20 to 30 minutes, but if your noodles are thinner than ours your time could be shorter.

Modifications for Younger Kids
If children struggle making long worms with the dough, consider giving them a clean pair of safety or play scissors. They can cut up tiny bits of the dough into their own version of pastini!

Modifications for Older Kids
Older kids (under supervision) can use tongs to lift the noodles out of the water, being careful not to burn themselves. This is a great opportunity to practice motor skills as the noodles can be very slippery. Kids can also play chef by creating a sauce for the family's meal.

Fruit Necklace

Accessories are a big hit at our house. We have gobs of friend bracelets and necklaces with homemade beads and ornate charms. While we love our *bling*, the best accessories are the ones that have an element of play.

This accessory doubles as a snack! The fun starts with your kids making their snack, wearing it, and then eating it. Girls and boys alike will enjoy getting to create and then eat their snack necklace made from stringing fruit onto dental floss.

Materials

+ Dental floss
+ Large plastic needle
+ 1 cup (145 g) berries and/or cut-up fruit (all should be bite size)

TIP

This is a great snack activity if you are traveling. Instead of using berries that might stain your car, have your kids create a pretzel necklace. They can make the necklace and then munch on it while traveling on the road.

Watch your kids as they thread the dental floss through the needle and add the fruit to their necklace.

Tie the necklace onto your child and enjoy!

Modifications for Younger Kids

Because eye-hand coordination can be challenging for small fingers, using fruit is a great introduction to sewing. Little ones may need help threading the needle.

Modifications for Older Kids

Encourage your older child to create patterns. Or think of other foods besides fruit that they could add to the necklace, such as bagel pieces, pretzels, cereal and so forth.

Greeting Card Puzzles

A window in our living room displays all the Christmas cards we receive each December, attached with a piece of tape. By Christmas, there are rows and rows of cards almost completely obscuring the view. I never know exactly what to do with them once the holiday is over. They are too pretty to throw away, but too many to keep. The same goes for birthday and special-event cards. That is the inspiration behind this activity to recycle cards into puzzles that kids can play over and over.

Materials

+ USED GREETING CARDS
+ SCISSORS
+ GLUE (OPTIONAL)

TIP

If the greetings within the card were special, cut down the card fold and glue the two pieces together so the image is on the front and the words are on the back, then cut the puzzle as a two-sided challenge.

Choose a greeting card that has a large picture on the front or trim a card down to just the image. Make puzzle-like cuts, starting with straight lines perpendicular to the edge for a simple puzzle.

For a more complex puzzle, glue back-to-back two greeting card images that are the same size and then cut the pieces. This will create a double-sided puzzle.

Modifications for Younger Kids

Laminate the card prior to cutting for more durability. Make the puzzle pieces large.

Modifications for Older Kids

You can have your child make the pieces smaller, or store several cards of puzzles together in the same bag. Half the activity will be sorting the various cards to begin the puzzles. You can also have older kids glue a collage of greeting cards onto a large piece of construction paper and then cut the entire collage into puzzle pieces.

Grape Structures

This "building set" combines two common kitchen items—grapes and toothpicks. It is surprisingly versatile. You can make simple shapes or build crazy 3-D sculptures and buildings. Or, if lots of toothpicks in one grape is more your speed, then just call it a porcupine.

Spend the afternoon building together and at the end, it doubles as a snack . . . just don't eat the toothpicks!

- -

Materials
+ GRAPES—LOTS OF THEM!
+ BOX OF TOOTHPICKS

TIP

Here is a fun prank idea using the grapes: Use the hole made by the toothpicks in the grapes to make an iris: stuff a raisin sliver into the center of the grape. You now have an "eye." Then freeze it in an ice cube. Stick the grape "eye" into your child's drink as a practical joke one day. They get a drink that is "watching" them.

Put the grapes in a pile and create geometric shapes by stuffing the toothpicks into the fruit. You can create circle dome houses, A-frame homes, tall towers and bridges. The sky is the limit!

Modifications for Younger Kids
If your child is having a hard time creating structures, try helping him or her make train tracks.

Modifications for Older Kids
Look up photos of some architectural landmarks. See if you can replicate them with the grapes and sticks.

Marshmallow Launcher

The story of David and Goliath is the best advertisement for slingshots. The thought of a child with a homemade weapon, doing what an army could not, is empowering. Our kids find twigs shaped like a Y and string it with a rubber band to shoot rocks across the backyard.

Unfortunately, our homemade weapons don't have the precision of David's and often a rock hurls in the wrong direction, creating play panic. This modification of the ancient slingshot is more reliable for firing and uses marshmallows for ammunition.

Materials

+ SCISSORS
+ SMALL DISPOSABLE PLASTIC CUPS
+ BALLOONS—ONE PER CUP
+ BAG OF MARSHMALLOWS (LARGE OR SMALL IS FINE)

TIP

If you don't like to use marshmallows as they contain a lot of sugar, replace them with pom-poms or Ping-Pong balls.

Start by cutting off the bottom of a plastic cup. This may be challenging if you are using a sturdy plastic version and should be done by adults.

Cut ½ inch (1 cm) off the top of the balloon and tie a knot in the end you use for blowing it up.

Spread the balloon over the now open bottom of the cup.

Place a large marshmallow or several mini marshmallows in the cup; pull back the balloon knot and release. Watch the marshmallows fly.

Modifications for Younger Kids
Younger kids need supervision around both balloons and marshmallows, so please use caution. Let them be your launch assistant.

Modifications for Older Kids
Older kids can chart the distance of a marshmallow launch and figure out which size marshmallows work the best for distance travel. Create a target and see which size can be controlled the best to hit the bull's-eye.

Masking Tape Road and Cityscape

A well-crafted pretend city is the perfect vacation. It doesn't cost any money to visit and you can control where you stay, what you eat and the tourist attractions that you see. If you want your city to have the Eiffel Tower, you can make that happen. If you want your city to have a roller coaster that goes through the Town Hall, you can create it. If you want your city to have ice-cream trucks on every corner, it is your call.

This activity uses painter's tape to create that pretend city. The city can start small in the living room and grow in population and square mileage to the kitchen and hall. Because it is painter's tape, city destruction and removal from REAL life is a breeze.

Materials

+ WIDE PAINTER'S TAPE
+ MARKER
+ TOY CARS AND/OR ACTION FIGURES

Use the tape to create roads, the shadowlike outlines of buildings and landmarks. Let kids get creative in city design—the couch may make the perfect mall. Think outside the box: let your cityscape crawl up the wall or across the furniture.

Modifications for Younger Kids

Instead of having your children create a full city, have them just create a track for their cars to drive or their dolls to walk on.

Modifications for Older Kids

Play a game of Treasure. Give them a map—have them recreate the "map" on the floor/wall. When they are finished, mark the map with a treasure location. Have children follow the map to get their car or figure to the destination.

TIP

Making a network of roads that your child can see from a "bird's-eye view" is a great way to practice direction commands like "Go right" or "Turn to your left" or "Make a U-turn and go back." Maybe you can create a diorama of your own neighborhood and practice telling directions with street names to help your child if he/she ever gets lost.

Paper Cup Castle

Growing up, I was sure that I was born into the wrong family or that somewhere in my family tree a royal bloodline was being held a secret. It just didn't seem right that I wasn't a true princess. I was born to be a princess who wore a sparkly crown and was in line to rule the land.

Surprisingly, no secrets were revealed and all my princess crown wearing and rule making were banished to the land of make-believe. Thankfully, the land of make-believe can be visited by any undiscovered prince and princess.

This simple activity starts as a package of plastic cups and a few pieces of paper. With some strategic building, it ends as a castle in the land of make-believe.

Materials
(to make one castle)

+ 5 TO 8 SHEETS OF PAPER
+ 100+ PLASTIC CUPS (LARGE CUPS WORK BEST)

TIP

Before play, have a peace treaty signed by all parties stating that neighboring kingdoms will not be invaded without the blessing of said kingdom. Knocking down castles is only fun if everyone is on board with the action.

To make the castle: Fold sheets of paper like an accordion to create strong paper platforms and bridges. Use cups as the stones of the castle.

Build the castle as large as possible with the available building materials.

Castles, walls, drawbridges, trees, townhouses and so many more things can be built out of paper cups and paper beams. The kingdoms can stand tall or spread out over the entire living room floor.

Modifications for Younger Kids
Replace the paper beams with strips of cardboard cut from leftover boxes. They make a flatter building surface.

Modifications for Older Kids
Challenge older kids to a minimum castle height requirement or have them scurry around the house, looking for additional building materials to fortify the castle.

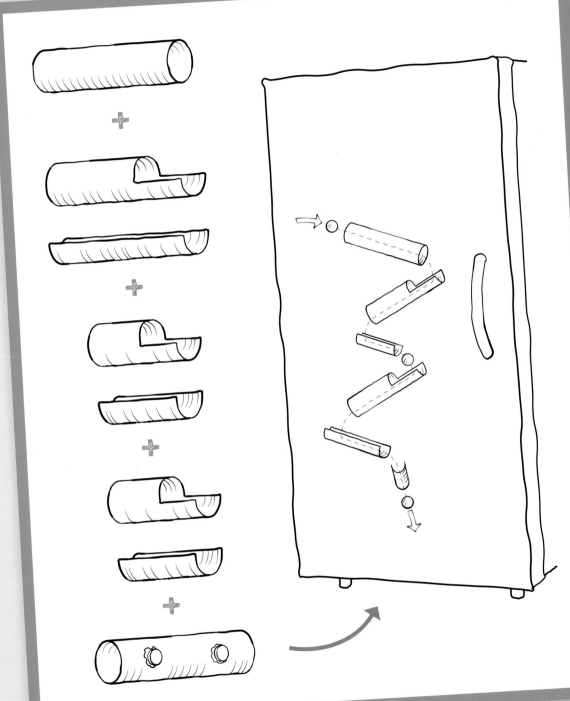

Ping-Pong Ball Run

A children's museum in our area has a wall that is made of metal. In buckets at the base of that wall are all sorts of pipes with magnets attached to one side to make tracks on the wall that will transport a ball with a little help from gravity. My kids love to play on the wall. Sometimes when we visit the museum, it is just to visit the wall.

Because my husband said a metal wall in our home was out of the question, I downsized this activity a bit to be recycled toilet paper and paper towel tubes stuck to the fridge.

Materials

+ Roll of magnetic tape
+ 6 to 10 empty paper towel and toilet paper tubes
+ Scissors
+ Masking tape
+ Ping-Pong balls

TIPS

Place a sticker over the flat surface of the attached magnet. This is done to protect the metal surface from scuffs the magnet can cause from sliding on the fridge.

Looking for another version of this activity? Check out the PVC Tube Play Wall activity (page 41) that is guaranteed to entertain your kids for a good hour.

Peel the backing off the magnetic tape and press the sticky side along the side of the tubes so that the tubes can be hung vertically and the magnets make contact with the metal.

Repeat for many different sizes of pieces to give variety to the Ping-Pong ball run.

On one piece, use masking tape to cover one end of a tube, so that you have a storage segment to allow the balls to be put away and stored on the fridge.

Modifications for Younger Kids

Set up a simple run at their level and hand them the Ping-Pong ball. It won't be long until they figure out how to make it go down the tube track.

Modifications for Older Kids

Older kids can find other things around the house to attach to the fridge as ball obstacles and tracks. They can cut the paper towel tubes into segments with windows, flaps and ends.

Pipe Cleaner Disguises

This activity is a mature version of peek-a-boo. Everyone is in on the joke that these really aren't disguises, but it is too fun to ruin with the truth. Grab some pipe cleaners and get ready for some laughter because this is going to get silly.

Materials

+ LOTS OF DIFFERENT COLORS AND SIZES OF PIPE CLEANERS
+ GLUE DOTS OR DOUBLE-SIDED TAPE

TIPS

Are you worried about the ends of the pipe cleaners poking one of your kids? Just fold the sharp end in and twist it inside itself. Your pipe cleaner should now be blunted and safer for small tots to enjoy.

This is a great activity for kids to do on a long car trip. Give them a collection of pipe cleaners and a mirror. They will giggle at one another as you drive.

Do you have extra pipe cleaners? Use some to create giant bubble wands to use along with bubble shooters (see page 56).

Create a unique disguise for yourself. We have some suggestions . . .

Spy Glasses
Take a pipe cleaner and make it into a spiral like a shell—you will need two. When finished, push the center of the spirals out to create a sort of cone. Attach the "cones" to the center of eyeglasses formed from pipe cleaners.

Antennae
Get your bug on! Create antennae and pretend to be an insect . . . or an alien. Use a couple of pipe cleaners to create a headband. Add antennae. Consider making the antennae from spirals or curling the ends of them.

Other pipe cleaner accessories you can make:

- Swords
- Hats
- Mustaches
- Cat whiskers
- Bushy eyebrows
- Flowers

Modifications for Younger Kids
Instead of having your children make or wear the disguises, print out a large picture of their face. Have your children visually "try on" the disguises on their picture.

Modifications for Older Kids
Have one child make the disguise for another child. Pick a character (e.g., a rock star, a small animal, a circus performer, etc.) and try to imagine disguises that they would use or that would define them. Become the character.

Playing Card Building Sets

We have drawers full of playing cards. Some were handed down from previous generations, some were picked up on travels, some were gifts and some were purchased at the last minute because, despite the drawers full of playing cards, we just couldn't find a full deck.

Recycle those tattered, incomplete decks into a building block set that is easily transported and endless in its play potential.

Materials
+ DECK OF PLAYING CARDS
  (CAN BE INCOMPLETE DECK)
+ SCISSORS

TIP
Despite the alteration of the cards, they will still fit back into the box, which makes these sets the perfect take-along toy.

Cut four slits in each card—1½ inches (4 cm) from each end of the long sides. The slits don't have to be deeper than ½ inch (1.3 cm), but they do need to be perpendicular to the edge.

Kids can use one or more sets to build large structures and sculptures. We are moving WAY beyond a house of cards!

Modifications for Younger Kids
Create a card-size building piece out of cardboard or heavy cardstock, because many playing cards can be a bit slick and hard for smaller fingers to manipulate.

Modifications for Older Kids
Make several decks of cards for a massive building experience.

Shadow Play

I remember vividly the day I really sat down and thought about my shadow. Well, it started out sitting, but then I got up and tried to trick it. I jumped and swayed and ducked and ran. No matter what I did, that shadow followed. I decided just to ignore it except for some covert peeks—a peek where only my eyes would move so my shadow wouldn't reflect that I was looking.

This activity gets the entire family involved because everyone has a shadow. Bring some life and jazz to your family's next dance party by playing with shadows as you dance.

Materials

+ PAINTER'S TAPE (TO HANG THE SHEET ON THE WALL)
+ LARGE WHITE SHEET—OR A BLANK WALL
+ DIRECTIONAL LIGHT
+ MUSIC

Use painter's tape to hang your sheet on the wall, then turn on the light. Explore with distance to see where you need to dance to get the crispest shadow of yourself. Turn on the music and watch your shadow dance.

Modifications for Younger Kids

Be sure to keep the light away from where the kids are dancing. The directional lights tend to get hot.

Modifications for Older Kids

With your children participating, make a list of some of your family's favorite activities. Throw the ideas into a hat and pick the ideas out. Try to reenact the scenes of your activities together as shadows. For an extra challenge, have them try to choreograph a scene between two people.

Pocket Puzzle Game

Grandma and Grandpa always had a very large and very challenging puzzle going on the dining room table. Grandma had it on a piece of cardboard so it could be moved in the event of a family gathering, but often the family gathering was around the puzzle. Every time someone walked by the table, he/she would pause to try to add another piece to the ever-evolving picture.

I love this next activity for the legacy of it. It is an open-ended puzzle where everyone can play. Using foam pieces, magnets and a metal mint container, you can create a puzzle to work together at home or on the go.

Materials
(to make one pocket puzzle)

+ A VARIETY OF COLORED STICKY FOAM SHEETS
+ MAGNETIC SHEET OR OLD MAGNETIC BUSINESS CARDS
+ GRAPH PAPER
+ SCISSORS
+ SMALL TIN BOX

TIP
Make a set of puzzle pieces for the fridge. Great for both holding to-do notes and to help entertain a child during meal preparation!

Peel the backing from the foam sheets and stick the magnets to the foam. We worked with small sections so we didn't waste all the magnets or foam. Lay the graph paper over the magnetic foam sheet and cut out a collection of shapes, following the lines in the graph paper. Repeat with the other colors of foam sheets. Try to think of a wide variety of shapes and designs, following the lines of the graph paper—so the puzzle will fit together when done. Tape a piece of graph paper inside the lid on the tin.

Have your kids play with their puzzle solo or as a group, taking turns adding a new piece. The goal is to fill the entire lid so that there aren't any blank spaces without pieces.

Modifications for Younger Kids
Make the pieces bigger and use a lunchbox instead of a small tin to hold the parts.

Modifications for Older Kids
Add the rule that they can't have pieces of the same color touch. Or have them try to create an image, like a house, inside the puzzle. You can also make this a timed event. Give them 3 minutes to completely fill the surface with no gaps. Shorten the time if they need more challenge. To make the game more complicated for older kids, make a rule that they can only place pieces of one color.

Sticky-Note Pom-pom Maze

This project transforms sticky notes into a maze that can be designed and constructed by a kid. The fun thing is that even though they designed the maze, it will still be a challenge to maneuver a pom-pom through it with a straw and some air power.

Materials

+ 2+ STACKS OF STICKY NOTES
+ TABLETOP SURFACE (OR THE FLOOR)
+ STRAWS—ONE PER CHILD PLAYING
+ A VARIETY OF DIFFERENT POM-POMS

TIPS

Wondering how to create a maze? Try filling in an entire 2 x 3-foot (61 x 91.5 cm) area with the sticky notes. When the entire "box" is filled, remove the notes to reveal the maze route.

Regulating breathing by blowing pom-poms is a great way to learn breath control. This is also a good "calm down." Breathing steadily will help mellow excited little bodies.

Create a maze track with the thin post-it notes (or masking tape). Line up the notes close together on a smooth surface, creating corners, turns and twists across the table.

Have your children pick out a straw and a pom-pom and start at the beginning of the maze. They need to blow their pom-pom to go through the maze without falling off the track. If they go outside of the lines of the "track" they need to take their pom-pom back to start and begin again.

Modifications for Younger Kids

Have your children work on blowing the straw evenly to get their pom-pom to move. This is a great way to work on breathing control. Our youngest tykes just liked blowing their pom-poms anywhere. They can have a simple start/finish line or a set of bases to get their pom-poms to.

Modifications for Older Kids

Cut the notes in half to make a narrower trail. Add some twists and turns in the maze, making it more difficult for kids to navigate their pom-pom around the barriers.

For a science twist, have your kids experiment. Is the pom-pom easier to control if they have a thinner straw? What happens when the size of the pom-pom changes?

PVC Pipe Tent

Wouldn't it be great if Tinker Toys were life-size so you could build a house and then live in it? The giant building possibilities would be endless!

I think that is why I love this project so much. Once you have created a PVC pipe set for play, it can be used and reused both inside and out to make anything you can dream up, including this homemade tent.

Materials

+ Ratcheting PVC cutter
+ 8 (10-foot [3 m] -long, ½-inch [1.3 cm] -diameter) PVC plumbing pipes
+ 10 (½-inch [1.3 cm] -diameter) 90-degree-elbow pieces
+ 12 (½-inch [1.3 cm] -diameter) T-shaped pieces
+ Permanent marker
+ Bedsheets

TIP

There is a lot of bang for your buck with a PVC pipe play set. The most expensive part was the ratcheting cutter, which cost approximately $10. The rest of the set was under $25.

Using the ratcheting PVC cutter, cut twelve 4-foot (122 cm) -long sections of pipe. These pieces will create the tent base.

The four roof segments need to create a right angle when placed together, so you will need to use the remaining long pieces to cut four segments that are 33⅞ inches (86 cm) long. Immediately label these pieces with a marker, making an "R" to remind yourself that they are the roof segments.

Using some of the leftover pieces cut a dozen 2-inch (5 cm) -long segments to use to create corners. Hang the bedsheets over the roof and wrap around the sides.

A recap: The pieces required for this tent:

• 12 (4-foot [122 cm]) -long segments

• 4 (33⅞-inch [86 cm]) -long segments labeled "R"

• 10 (90-degree) elbows

• 12 T pieces

• 12 (2-inch [5 cm]) -long segments

Modifications for Younger Kids

If only smaller kids are included in this project, it would be wise to cut all measurements in half and make a miniature version of this tent. This is the perfect family activity to help build and then the kids can play.

Modifications for Older Kids

Have older kids design a structure and then create directions to make it. The directions outlined above were devised with some help of the Pythagorean theorem and my fifth grader's math skills.

PVC Tube Play Wall

Chain reactions are not always the easy way to the finish line, but they are great entertainment. Accomplishing something simple through complex actions was the basis of Rube Goldberg's inventions. He created elaborate means to a common task with one step triggering the next.

This activity puts the power of complex actions to accomplish a common result in the hands of kids in the form of interchangeable PVC pipes. They can harness gravity and set and reset the steps toward the goal. They think they know what will happen next, but are often surprised!

Materials

+ A VARIETY OF 2¼-INCH (5.5 CM) PVC CONNECTORS
+ DRILL
+ PLASTIC FUNNEL
+ 2-INCH (5 CM) –DIAMETER SUCTION CUPS—ONE FOR EACH CONNECTOR
+ CONTAINER THAT FITS ON WINDOWSILL
+ MEASURING CUP(S)
+ DRIED BEANS, BEADS, SEEDS, COLD CEREAL, ETC.

TIP

Set up the tubes in the tub for a wet, water run.

Choose a variety of 2¼-inch (5.5 cm) PVC connectors. We used seven connectors—three straight, two obtuse angles, one T piece and one right angle—and a plastic funnel.

Drill a hole in the plastic funnel and each of the connectors. Fill each hole with a suction cup.

On a window at kid level, arrange the first version of a "fall wall"—create a path or two that cascades from the top, emptying into the container sitting on the windowsill. Test the chain reaction with a cupful of beans, small pom-poms, marbles or even breakfast cereal.

Kids can work together to change the path of the falling material and experiment with measuring cups of different ingredients to find out how things fall.

Modifications for Younger Kids

Depending on the age of the child, choose an ingredient that is safe for play. Wash the Play Wall elements in the dishwasher, clean the space around the bottom and allow only cereal as the ingredient for those who are likely to put things in their mouth.

Modifications for Older Kids

Create a smaller "target" inside the windowsill container with a measuring cup for them to fill with a specific amount of a specific ingredient. Have older children design a pathway that divides into a specific number of trails at the bottom. Give older children a challenge to "fix" the path designed by a smaller child in two moves.

Sensory Bag Collection

Sensory bags are curious things. They are a mixture of textures and feeling sensations sealed into a mess-proof play experience. For some kids who shy away from messy hands, it is a way they can be introduced to what a mess feels like. For others, it is another way to play that won't end in a trip to the bathtub for a full body wash-down.

The ingredients usually include a liquid and solids that aren't normally found together, for a unique touch adventure. We have collected several of our favorites that can be created with things you already have at home. Feel free to make substitutions and enhancements customized for what your child loves.

Materials
+ ASSORTED SENSORY ITEMS (SEE SUGGESTIONS)
+ RESEALABLE PLASTIC FREEZER BAGS
+ CLEAR PACKING TAPE

Add the sensory elements inside the bag, filling it just enough so when the bag is lying on its side, the contents completely cover the surface in a layer less than 1 inch (2.5 cm) deep. Try to remove all the air from the bag. Seal the bag tightly and reinforce the closure with tape.

Lumpy Ocean
Combine blue hair gel and Styrofoam bits (could be stuffed animal filling or packing peanuts cut into small pieces). This bag is delightfully squishy and cool to the touch with soft bumps to explore.

Mess-free Paint
Add paint in your child's favorite color inside a bag and then give him/her a cotton swab to draw pictures or practice handwriting. The pressure of the swab will cause the paint to part, leaving a magical writing surface. Use this canvas as a wipe-off board for a game of "What am I drawing?"

Flower Texture
Combine clear hair gel and some leftover silk flowers without stems. This bag is pretty to look at, fun to feel and a great pool or bath toy.

Modifications for Younger Kids
Very young kids need to be supervised around plastic bags. If your child tends to handle things roughly, double the bag and add an extra layer of tape!

Modifications for Older Kids
While this is usually thought of as an activity for younger kids, older kids can create a themed bag with their favorite items. Adding a base of thick liquid or gel can make this a fun desk accessory with stress-relieving properties!

Straw Glider

In my mind, a toy airplane resembles the real thing—two wings, a nose and often a tail. If it flies, it looks like that. This paper glider is different. It doesn't look like anything that would fly at all.

So, grab a straw and a piece of paper and build the glider that defies gravity, as I know it. You will be pleasantly surprised as your "UFO-like" creation sails.

Materials
(to make a single glider)

+ 1 SHEET OF CARDSTOCK OR ANOTHER STIFF PAPER
+ SCISSORS
+ TAPE
+ DRINKING STRAW

TIP

Are your kids bored at the restaurant? Recycle straws and beverage cozies to create these flying masterpieces—just be sure to leave the restaurant before you test them in flight!

Cut the paper into two strips. Tape each strip into a paper hoop with one of the hoops being slightly larger than the other. Then tape the hoops onto the straw.

Set up a series of bases throughout the house. Pillows work great as bases. Have each child throw a glider at the first base. If the glider reaches the first base, that kid can advance to it and on his next turn throw toward the next base. The person who completes all the bases first is the winner.

Modifications for Younger Kids
Younger kids can be given a zone of grace around each base appropriate with their ability—so instead of needing to touch the base with the glider, they can be within a 2-foot (61 cm) radius.

Modifications for Older Kids
Older kids can experiment with different glider designs. Does the glider go farther with bigger hoops or smaller ones? What if the hoops were closer together or farther apart? Can the glider fly with three hoops?

Stuffed Animal Marionette

One of my favorite movie scenes is the puppet show in *The Sound of Music*. The elaborate puppet show was performed by the kids for the rest of the family. There was a gold and red stage with curtains and fancy marionettes. The children stood above, manipulating all the action with long and invisible strings. I can still see the lonely goatherd and goat dancing in front of the mountain backdrop. Lay ee odl layee odl-oo.

Inspired by the Von Trapps but without the Austrian château budget, this activity breathes life into stuffed animals.

Materials
(to transform one stuffed animal into a puppet)

+ 2 RULERS
+ BALL OF YARN
+ SCISSORS
+ STUFFED ANIMAL
+ BINDER CLIP OR STAPLER

Make an X with the rulers and tie the middle securely with yarn, leaving a length of yarn hanging from the middle. At each end of the four points, attach another strand of yarn, through the hole near the end of each ruler.

Tie the four strings from the points to the arms and legs of the animal. Attach the middle string to the back of the stuffed animal's head by using a binder clip or stapling it securely.

Holding on to the rulers, tip in different directions to make the stuffed animal walk and dance.

Modifications for Younger Kids
Keeping the yarn strands short will keep them less tangled during play.

Modifications for Older Kids
You may need to buy rulers in bulk because creating an entire cast can revive interest in animals that may have been hiding under the bed for years!

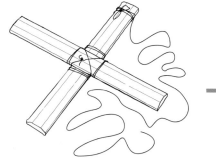  

Tin Can Drums

There is something about making noise that is simply delightful to kids. Toy manufacturers have caught on to this, resulting in increasingly frantic toys' blasting bells, whistles, talking and singing accompanied by a full band. These toys will end up quickly confiscated just for a moment of peace by normally calm parents.

This activity takes away the bells, whistles, talking and full band to go back to the basics of sound—the drum. When kids can experiment with sounds in a quiet environment, they can start recognizing the different tones. Grab a tin can and some balloons—we are making a drum!

Materials
(to make a single drum)

+ BALLOONS OF VARIOUS COLORS
+ SCISSORS
+ EMPTY CANS (OR OTHER CYLIN-DRICAL METAL CONTAINERS)
+ RUBBER BANDS
+ SPOONS AND STICKS—WOODEN SPOONS AND CHOPSTICKS WORK GREAT

TIP

Are you looking for more fun? Use the finished tin can drum as a small trampoline for vaulting objects, or small action figures, into the air.

Cut off the elongated portion of a balloon (where you blow into) and stretch it over the end of a can. Choose a complementary color of balloon and repeat the process, with the addition of clipping a few holes in the second balloon. Secure both with a rubber band to the tin can.

Make several different drums. Using different-size tin cans or other cylinders can help create different sounds.

Using wooden spoons or chopsticks, play each drum to hear the different sounds each makes. You can even just use your hands and see how the tone changes. Create a family band!

Modifications for Younger Kids
Because balloon parts can be dangerous, substitute waxed paper or cellophane for the balloon. Using an empty oatmeal container makes a larger drum, and it has no sharp edges to be concerned about.

Modifications for Older Kids
Older kids can use different types of materials to create a drum surface and different drum barrels. Adding rice, dried beans, marbles or other items to the drum barrel can also affect sound.

Tree Wood Blocks

Building is great for growing brains. The act of stacking items helps kids develop spatial awareness and understand the relationship between cause and effect. Our kids love stacking blocks of all shapes and sizes.

As our children have grown, their building interests have expanded but never waned. They love to create elaborate towers, houses and cityscapes. Some days it feels like there are not enough blocks in the world to entertain their creativity. We were thrilled when a tree in our backyard needed to be cut down: we could create a whole new set of blocks!

Materials

+ 2 OR 3 TREE LIMBS, ROUGHLY 3 INCHES (7.5 CM) IN DIAMETER
+ TABLE SAW (WE USED AN ELECTRIC ONE)
+ SANDPAPER (COARSE AND FINE GRAIN)
+ GLOVES FOR YOUR CHILD
+ BUTCHER BLOCK OIL (LINSEED, OR FOOD-GRADE MINERAL OIL OR ANYTHING MARKETED AS SAFE FOR FOOD SURFACES—AND THEREFORE A CHILD'S MOUTH)

TIPS

These blocks make a great gift for holidays! Place a couple dozen disks into a box with some woods animals for the child in your life to enjoy. For an adult gift, make more narrow disks and gift them as coasters.

Cut disks from your tree limbs, using the power saw. Older children might be able to help by marking off how long they would like the blocks to be—a wide variety of sizes makes building a fun challenge.

After you have cut the disks, use sandpaper to smooth any rough edges. This is the hard part. For the best blocks, you will want to give your wood a chance to dry out and age. Stack your cut blocks in a corner of the garage, away from moisture, and allow them to harden. This is especially important if you used wood from a recently live tree.

Once the wood has aged for a month or two, sand the edges again. Put gloves on your children and give them a clean rag that has been lightly dipped in butcher block oil. Have them rub the oil into the blocks. This will help preserve them.

Modifications for Older Kids

Have your child collect a variety of small sticks at the same time that you are cutting up the tree. They can use these in coordination with the blocks to build their structures. Add some props to their building play: yarn and a bandana, as well as figures and animals, will open the doors to endless hours of pretend play.

Modifications for Younger Kids

While the creation of these toy blocks is best suited for older kids, playing with them is something kids of all ages will enjoy.

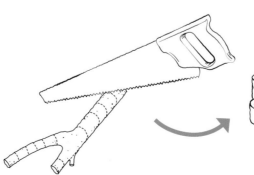

Tin Can Jump

The satisfaction in mastering something difficult by yourself, as a child, is hard to top. Repeating something over and over again until it can be done may seem like work to the outside world, but in the mind of the persistent child it is worth it when success is achieved. In today's childhood, many of these solo accomplishments are achieved through video games and practicing organized sports' skills.

This activity takes a step back into generations past for a simple gross motor skill developed with a solo jump rope using a tin can.

Materials
(to make one jump rope)

+ EMPTY MEDIUM-SIZE TIN CAN
+ SANDPAPER OR STURDY TAPE
+ HAMMER
+ THICK NAIL
+ ROPE

TIP
This can be an indoor rainy-day activity—just cover the can first with felt or faux craft fur to decrease the sound and any damage that the can could cause to flooring.

Sand down any sharp edges on the tin can with sandpaper or cover them with sturdy tape. Using a hammer and nail, create a hole in the end. Thread both ends of a rope through the hole and secure with a knot.

Step one foot inside the rope circle and swing it around, jumping over the moving can with the other leg.

Modifications for Younger Kids
This can be modified to a two-person game for kids who are too young to coordinate it solo. Adults or older children, who can successfully jump the rope alone, can have younger children stand at their side next to their jump rope leg. They can participate by jumping over the moving can as it flies underneath them.

Modifications for Older Kids
Older kids can be given challenges, such as a number of jumps in a row to achieve or once one side is coordinated, switch legs and master the other side as well.

Toe Painting with a Paint Recipe

My first exposure to finger painting was in kindergarten. Parents had been instructed to send an art smock (one of Dad's old shirts) so that we could paint at school. In my mind, that meant paintbrushes and canvases, but when the finger paints were brought out to paint on a large, paper-covered easel, I was hooked.

The paint was so cool to touch and fingers can manipulate paint in a different way than does a brush. This activity increases the sensory experience and uses toes to paint. Toe painting is a new way to explore with color!

Materials

+ SHAVING CREAM
+ TEMPERA PAINT IN A VARIETY OF COLORS
+ LIGHT CORN SYRUP—1 TEASPOON (5 ML) PER COLOR (OPTIONAL)
+ WET TOWEL (FOR QUICK CLEANUP)

TIP

Do you have a grimy surface on your craft table? Use plain shaving cream and add a pile to the table. Let your kiddos play and smear the pile of shaving cream. The leftover bits of dried glue and paint will come up as your children play, making cleanup easier.

Make a pile of shaving cream that is roughly a cup (about 230 g). Add a squirt of color and mix until you have the desired color. Add a teaspoon (5 ml) of corn syrup. If you don't care about the finished product as much you can leave out the corn syrup. The corn syrup gives the paint a semigloss finish.

Paint colors can be mixed in plastic cups to create a whole bunch of colored paint batches. Turn the cups upside down to fully appreciate the thick and creamy consistency that is nearly impossible to spill!

Let your children paint a picture with bare feet. Have a bucket of water and a towel ready for when they are finished.

Modifications for Younger Kids

Instead of "toe painting," paint with their fingers. If you are working on prewriting skills with your kids, have them use a paintbrush. It will help them develop the hand control needed when it is time for them to begin writing. Do you have a child who puts everything in his/her mouth? Consider using plain yogurt combined with food coloring as the paint, instead of the shaving cream and tempera in this recipe.

Modifications for Older Kids

Add some challenge and ask your kids to paint with their bums in the air—they will have fun trying to figure out how to write without "resting." It is a great way for them to both develop core strength and practice controlled movements (needed for many sports).

This is a fun group activity for an art-themed party. Lay a long piece of butcher paper out and watch the kids paint with their feet.

Wooden Block Townhouses

Saturday afternoons are family time at our house. We have a set of wooden blocks that always seem to make their way to the middle of the living room and it isn't long before the adults usually take over and make a structure tall enough to touch the ceiling. Kids are welcome to help on the bottom parts, but as the skyscraper grows, the kids know to stand farther and farther away. It is for their protection because after the skyscraper successfully touches the ceiling, a pivotal base piece is pulled out followed by a tremendous crash as wooden blocks fall from the sky.

These wooden block townhouses are the perfect complement to the toys kids already have and love. In our case, this makes a lovely suburban play set while the dangerous city is being constructed and destructed.

Materials

+ Small scraps from two-by-fours
+ Sandpaper
+ Painter's tape
+ White paint
+ Paintbrushes
+ Paint markers

First, sand any rough edges on the wooden blocks with sandpaper. Using painter's tape, tape off square and rectangular windows on the wood block surface.

Paint the "windows" white. Peel off the tape and let dry. Once dry, use paint markers to outline the window details and let dry.

Your wooden block townhouses are all ready for play. You can stack them on top of one another to create a high-rise, or line them up along a street and grab the toy cars.

Modifications for Younger Kids

Younger kids can do all the painting where tape is involved. These are great toys for even small kids.

Be sure to use nontoxic paint, in case smaller players put the blocks in their mouth.

Modifications for Older Kids

Let older kids design more elaborate townhouse decor. Access to a saw could result in different roof pitches. More colors could create a townhouse row reminiscent of San Francisco's finest streets.

CRAFTS

Making something with a child is about the process, not the product. The memories are made from the collective energy of creation. The finished craft is an experience souvenir.

Holly's Pick: I adore the Shake-It-Up Ink (page 88) because over time, markers become very dear to me and this is a way to use them all the way up!

Rachel's Pick: Kick the Can Art (page 78) is a great way for kids to be active while creating art! The finished product looks a bit like Pollock's works. We have several on our walls.

Bubble Prints

Bubbles and childhood are a perfect match. They require a surprising amount of concentration to create. The perfect bubble is one that is a bit bigger or elongated or has a particularly bright rainbow or holds together longer. Actually, the perfect bubble seems to be the current one!

This activity uses bubbles to create art prints. It includes our favorite bubble recipe and a fun use of recycled water bottles to create a bubble rainbow.

Materials
(to make one bubble shooter)

+ 9 TO 12 DRINKING STRAWS
+ RUBBER BAND
+ BROAD PLASTIC CUP
+ MULTIPLE SHEETS OF PAPER

STRONGEST BUBBLES
(to make about 1 ½ cups [360 ml] bubble solution)

+ 1 CUP (235 ML) WATER
+ ⅓ CUP (80 ML) LIQUID DISH DETERGENT (NOT CONCENTRATED; IF CONCENTRATED, USE SLIGHTLY LESS)
+ 3 TABLESPOONS (45 ML) CORN SYRUP
+ 10 TO 15 DROPS FOOD COLORING

It is best to stir the ingredients to mix them, not shake. Let it sit overnight for the best results. We split our recipe into multiple baby food jars and then added food dye for our printing craft.

Grab a handful of straws and secure them together with a rubber band. We found that five or six straws worked best.

Dip one end into the bubble solution placed into a plastic cup broad enough to accommodate the straw bundle. Blow lots of bubbles!

Hold the end of the shooter over a piece of paper and see what happens on the paper as the colored bubbles pop. Let dry.

Modifications for Younger Kids
Instead of using dish detergent to create the bubbles, make them pain-free by using tear-free baby wash. This way, if your child gets a bubble in an eye it won't sting.

Younger kids who might inhale with the straw in their mouth vs. exhale should continue to use a bubble wand until the coordination is mastered. No one wants a mouthful of bubbles!

Modifications for Older Kids
Cut the bottom off a water bottle. Put a dish rag over the opening and use a rubber band to secure that to the bottle. Dip the rag into the bubble juice and blow on the "mouth" of the bottle. The result should be a "snake" of bubbles.

Use your bubble-printed paper to write a card to a friend or family member you haven't seen in a long time—you can also use bubble prints on butcher paper to create your own wrapping paper for gifts.

Cootie Catcher of Love

The magic of origami is simple. You take a flat, common piece of paper and with a few strategic folds it is transformed into a 3-D object with moving parts. As a big fan of making something out of nothing, I am fascinated by the mysteries of paper potential.

This easy folding project is a perfect rainy-day activity to help connect and tell your children how much they are loved and appreciated.

Materials
(to make one Cootie Catcher)

+ SHEET OF PAPER ROUGHLY 8 INCHES (20.5 CM) SQUARE
+ A VARIETY OF MARKERS OR COLORED PENCILS

Fold the corners of the square into the center to form a smaller square.

Turn the paper over, so the "flaps" face "down."

Fold the corners again into the middle of the page.

Bend the seams so the cootie catcher "works."

Put something that describes your child on each section of the catcher. The first large flat area would have four unfinished statements like "You make me smile . . .," "You are so sweet . . .," "I love it when you . . .," or "My favorite thing to do with you is . . .."

Inside each of those flaps fill with words that finish that statement.

After it is decorated, stick your fingers into the flaps and unfold it. Ask the kids to pick which decorated flap they prefer.

Modifications for Younger Kids
Have Mom or Dad (or an older participant) fold the catcher and the younger child can be in charge of decorations. The words can be simplified or simple pictures drawn for direct actions such as: hug, hold my hand, smile, jump and so on.

Modifications for Older Kids
This is great for a slumber party activity. Each child can create a catcher of love. Sit in a circle and pass the catcher to one another. Write something nice about the person whose catcher you are holding; keep passing until each child has written something nice about the other children. This makes the perfect party favor.

Craft Stick Puzzles

In my room, under my bed was a shoebox full of treasures. I collected tiny things that I found or purchased with cherished allowance dollars. There was a set of nested paper boxes where the largest one was no bigger than 2 inches (5 cm) across that a friend made and decorated. There was a tiny clay teapot that was given to me for my birthday. There was one of those plastic mazes with a ball bearing. Each held value much bigger than its size.

I believe if I had made something like these craft stick puzzles back then, it would have been added to that box. Create a puzzle using craft sticks and then place a rubber band around them for storage—the perfect fit for any treasure box.

Materials
(to make one puzzle)

+ 6 TO 8 WIDE CRAFT STICKS
+ WIDE PAINTER'S OR MASKING TAPE
+ MARKERS OR PAINT

TIP

Make a quiet-time bag for naps-on-the-run. We have all had to do an errand at the worst time of day—naptime. Calming activities are a great alternative when naps are unavailable. Consider adding these puzzle sticks, the Dry-Erase Doodles (page 13) and the Baggie Maze (page 10) to your "quiet" bag.

Place craft sticks next to one another on a table, making a blank canvas as wide as you want your puzzle to be. Using a piece of painter's tape, secure them together. Turn over and decorate with markers or paint.

When done with the puzzle decor, release the sticks from the tape. Try to put the puzzle back together, restoring the picture you drew.

Modifications for Younger Kids
The simpler the picture, the easier it will be to put together. Consider making one gigantic geometric shape that your toddler or preschooler needs to put together.

Modifications for Older Kids
Have older kids repeat the process on the blank side of the puzzle with the same colors they used in the original picture. This will make it more difficult to put together either side as a complete picture. You can also make multiple puzzles and mix the sticks together.

Bathtub Art with Recipe

There are two types of people in the world: those who take baths and those who don't. I don't mean the latter are unwashed, but they certainly don't appreciate the luxury of a good tub bath. Kids who enjoy a bath will love this project and those who don't might just be converted.

This art project uses DIY bathtub paint and a large tub tile canvas to create art.

Materials

+ SEVERAL COLORS OF HOMEMADE BATHTUB PAINT (BELOW)
+ PAINTBRUSH(ES)
+ BATHTUB

**HOMEMADE BATHTUB PAINT
(to make about 1 1/2 cups [355 ml] paint)**

+ MEDIUM-SIZE BOWL
+ 1/2 CUP (64 G) CORNSTARCH
+ 1/2 CUP (120 ML) BOILING WATER
+ 1 CUP (235 ML) DISH DETERGENT
+ LIQUID FOOD COLORING

In the bowl, stir the cornstarch into the hot water until it is dissolved and has a pasty consistency. Add the soap and stir until there are no chunks. Add the desired color of food coloring. Store in an airtight container. Stir well before use.

This paint is easy enough to use with both brushes and fingers, depending on the artist's preference.

It can be washed away when bathtime is over and the mess will just go down the drain.

Modifications for Younger Kids
Just painting in the tub without a picture goal in mind is fun. Kids can even use the paint to paint themselves.

Modifications for Older Kids
Paint tub tiles different colors to create a very large pixel art installation. This can be planned ahead of time, using graph paper.

TIP
If you are worried about your child having a reaction to the dish detergent in the paint, you can replace the dish detergent with any clear shampoo that your family prefers.

No-Sew No-Glue Tutu

One of the best things about being a girl is that accessorizing can be an art form. There is no reason to step out into the world with ordinary clothes when tiaras, tutus and princess attire are at your fingertips. Dressing isn't for warmth and protection. Dressing is for expression.

What we love about this homemade tutu is that it is perfect for those of us who haven't developed sewing skills. A simple slipknot attaches the tutu fluff for a custom look.

Materials
(to make one tutu)

+ Scissors
+ Elastic long enough to fit around the child's waist
+ Fabric and ribbon scraps—lots of them!
+ Tulle strips—cut 4 inches (10 cm) wide

Cut a piece of elastic long enough to wrap around your child's waist. Knot it. Make sure it is tight enough that the skirt won't fall off but loose enough to pull on and off easily. If you leave a "tail" on the knot, you can retie it to make the skirt bigger as your kids grow.

Take a fabric or ribbon scrap and create a slipknot over the waistband to attach it. The tails of the scrap can be even, or if you want more of a free-form look, they can be staggered. Repeat until you have the desired skirt fullness.

Have fun planning the different fabrics and ribbons to make your skirt. You can do a theme—like green or tan strips to make a "luau" skirt, or tie small jingle bells to the bottom of the strips for a musical dress.

Modifications for Younger Kids
Younger kids will love watching the tutu grow as each fabric strip is added. Have them choose which scrap is added next.

Modifications for Older Kids
Have your child create the knots. Older girls may find that this slipknot technique can be used for crafting custom headbands, bracelets and ponytail holders.

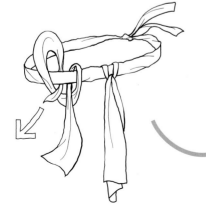

Painting on Crayons and Gel Paint

Painting and coloring are often thought about as separate projects, but this activity combines the two for a delightfully colorful two-step art process. The fun thing about this activity is that it is well suited for artists of all ages. Even the youngest kids can get involved with some crayon banging on paper that is transformed into a masterpiece with a simple homemade gel paint recipe.

Materials

+ WHITE CONSTRUCTION PAPER
+ LIGHT OR BRIGHTLY COLORED CRAYONS
+ PAINTBRUSH OR SPONGES

GEL PAINT
(to make about ¼ cup [60 ml] of paint)

+ 4 TABLESPOONS (60 ML) HAIR GEL
+ 5 TO 15 DROPS FOOD COLORING

TIP

We prefer using lighter colors of crayon and darker colors of paint over the crayon, for the best effect.

The ratio of dye to hair gel can be altered to get a more colorful paint result. This paint will keep for months in an airtight container.

We love the ease of making this paint—and cleanup is a breeze. Even if the paint has dried on, it will wash off the brushes easily. It is perfect for group events!

Start with a plain piece of paper and create a crayon drawing, using different colors and filling in different areas with crayon strokes. It is best to use contrasting crayons from the color of the paint. For example, if you are going to paint the background with dark paint, color with light, bright colors.

After your children have filled the pages with the crayon drawing, have them wipe the project with a single color of paint. Lightly buff the artwork afterward to watch the crayon coloring "pop" out. Beautiful!

Modifications for Younger Kids

Please be aware that this recipe is not edible, so close supervision may be required. To make this into an edible recipe, use plain gelatin mix instead of the hair gel. Gelatin paint is not smooth, so it's better for finger painting; also, note that it does not store as well.

Modifications for Older Kids

Explore color theory with your kids. Kids can make choices on color combinations that will be complementary, based on the color wheel, or choose to work on a monochromatic masterpiece.

Decorated Dishes

The kids in our house all have their own mugs. Having something in the kitchen that is "just theirs" is a special treat. Each child designed and created the custom mugs. It makes it easier to set the table or figure out who might have left a dish on the kitchen counter.

Having a special plate, bowl or mug makes mealtime more fun. This activity personalizes a mug or dish. These are treasured at home or make great gifts for family and friends.

Materials

+ Scissors
+ Piece of paper
+ Crayons or markers
+ Clear ovenproof mugs or dishes
+ Rubbing alcohol
+ Permanent oil markers

TIP

If you are using white mugs or dishes, have the children lightly color their outline with a crayon. Don't have them color it in; use the oil pens to color in the picture. Keep in mind that the oil pens will not color on top of crayon.

Cut pieces of plain paper slightly smaller than the surface of the mug you will be decorating. We used an 8½ x 11-inch (20.5 x 28 cm) piece of paper folded into four sections. Have the kids draw/color/paint/doodle on the paper, creating the design that will be traced onto the mug. Kids can create several designs and then choose the best one.

Prepare the mug's surface by wiping with rubbing alcohol to remove any oil. Even a greasy fingerprint will cause the paint to not set properly.

Secure the paper on the inside of the mug and then trace the design with permanent oil markers on the outside.

Leave the mugs overnight for the paint to fully dry. Then put them in a cold oven and set the temperature for 350°F (180°C or gas mark 4) and bake for an hour. Turn off the oven and let the mugs slowly cool before removing them. If exposed to rapidly changing temperature, many mugs will crack.

Modifications for Younger Kids

Keep younger kids away from permanent oil markers because they can stain the skin. Have them draw the original and have an adult transfer the art to the mug for the children.

Modifications for Older Kids

Let them draw directly onto the surface of the mugs or dishes. If they make a mistake, encourage them to incorporate that mistake into the artwork.

Clay Recipe for Bead Making

You can create your own ceramic-like clay—it is great for molds, for sculpting and for making beads—using ingredients commonly found in the kitchen! This is better than a trip to the ceramics studio.

Materials

AIR-DRY CLAY
(to make 3 ½ cups [about 700 g] clay)

+ 1 CUP (128 G) CORNSTARCH
+ 2 CUPS (442 G) BAKING SODA
+ 1 ½ CUPS (355 ML) WATER
+ 1 TABLESPOON (15 G) CREAM OF TARTAR

BRACELET OR NECKLACE

+ AIR-DRY CLAY
+ TOOTHPICK
+ METALLIC ACRYLIC PAINT
+ 12 TO 18-INCH (30.5 TO 45.5 CM) –LONG PIECE OF STRONG STRING (BRACELET OR NECKLACE LENGTH)
+ PLASTIC SEWING NEEDLE

TIP
Substituting elastic for string makes it easier to wear, but just a bit more challenging to string.

Mix the clay ingredients in a medium-size saucepan over medium heat on the stove top. Stir constantly. It is finished cooking when the clay pulls away from the sides of the pan (it should be the consistency of dough). Try to use it the day you make the dough; in a pinch you can store in an airtight container and revitalize it with a spray of water prior to use.

Take small equal portions and roll them into spheres. Use a toothpick to create a hole through the middle of the sphere. Roll the newly formed beads in metallic paint. Let air-dry overnight.

String the dried beads onto the string (the string can be doubled to strengthen it) in the pattern of choice. Tie the ends together a little bigger than wrist circumference so that the bracelet can be pulled on over the hand.

Modifications for Younger Kids
Use a plastic needle (a dull one) for younger kids to use to aid in stringing the beads.

Modifications for Older Kids
Letting kids get creative with bead size, shape and color allows them to make a unique accessory.

DIY Roll-Up Crayons

A special treasure in your school pencil box is a reminder from home throughout the day that you are part of a family that loves you. This fancy school supply is something that likely no one else at school will have—it will give your kids a smile and remind them of the fun time they had making it at home.

All you need is used glue stick containers and old crayons to create a twist-up crayon that is sure to make kids smile. Or upcycle extra-wide straws—they are super hard to fill, but the finished product of an ultralong crayon is awesome! Medicine bottles make perfectly sized crayons for toddlers (be sure to wash thoroughly before recycling).

Materials

+ Empty clean glue stick tubes
+ Tape
+ Sheet of paper
+ Muffin tin
+ Cupcake liners
+ Old broken crayons
+ Paper to wrap the finished sticks (optional, if gifting)

Clean out the inside of the empty glue stick with soap and water and let dry. Tape paper around the glue stick container to cover the label. Our kids love making their roll-up crayons pretty.

Line a muffin tin with the cupcake liners. Use each wrapper for a different color. Peel the crayons and place in the cupcake liners with like-colored crayons.

Preheat your oven to 350°F (180°C or gas mark 4). Leave the muffin tin in the oven for 8 to 10 minutes, until the crayons are fully melted. Pour the melted color from the cupcake liner into the empty glue container. Let cool.

Modifications for Younger Kids

Obviously, any step that has anything to do with oven use or hot melted wax crayons needs to be completed by an adult. Younger kids can design colors to go into each glue container by combining primary colors. Have younger kids decorate construction paper wrappers for the glue containers.

Modifications for Older Kids

Older kids can make swirled colors by adding different colors of crayons together and lightly swirling the colors together as it cools.

Freezer Paper Stencils

One Christmas I made decorated pillowcases for each of my relatives. Each pillowcase was stretched over a piece of cardboard and painted, using fabric paint and stencils. I set them in a row on the floor, propped up against the wall to dry. That was when the next-door neighbor's cat showed up. The cat proceeded to walk along the wall, dragging his tail through my works of art while I screamed and started planning new presents.

So put out the cat, because we are painting pillowcases, or T-shirts, dish towels, tote bags and so on—the options are endless! This simple craft uses freezer paper to create stencils for kids to use to customize fabric items.

Materials
+ Pencil or pen
+ Roll of freezer paper
+ Scissors
+ Cardboard
+ T-shirt or other fabric like a pillowcase
+ Fabric paint and paintbrushes

TIP
Why use paper gift wrap that is just discarded? Consider wrapping your gift in a decorated pillowcase the next time you are going to a birthday party.

Trace a shape onto freezer paper and cut out. The simpler the design, the better the outcome will be. Cut out the stencil.

Out of cardboard, create a flat surface to place under the first layer of fabric. Place the stencil on the fabric and outline it with crazy strokes of fabric paint.

Allow the paint to dry a bit before removing the stencil, to prevent seepage and drips. Pull off the stencil and admire the transformation.

If you are making a pillowcase, consider painting with glow-in-the-dark paint over your artwork. Your kids will love to look at their pillow art as they go to sleep.

Modifications for Younger Kids
Let kids choose the design for older participants to create a stencil. Younger kids can help outline and pull off the stencil after the paint has dried.

Squeezing a bottle of paint is a good fine-motor exercise. Finding a fabric paint bottle that is a good size for your child's hand will aid in coordination of painting.

Modifications for Older Kids
Older kids can be let loose on this project to design and create as they wish. Creating a set of matching pillowcases for an upcoming slumber party or gifting their best friend with a matching pillow can be a lot of fun!

Homemade Paint Recipe for Mask Making

One of my kids dressed as a Blue Power Ranger for eight months. Each morning he would get up and put on blue clothing (only blue clothing) and then cover it with the Power Ranger costume. The mask was a flat plastic circle with an elastic band that usually sat on top of his head, ready to pull down for any necessary superhero actions.

Some kids need to dress up. It is part of developing who they are growing to be. I can report that I haven't seen the Power Ranger costume for years, but occasionally he still wears blue.

This activity upcycles cereal boxes into handmade masks painted with a homemade paint recipe known to be used by the masters.

Materials
(to make one mask)

+ A VARIETY OF CHALK STICKS (GREAT USE OF LEFTOVER SCRAPS FROM SIDEWALK CHALK)
+ BOWL
+ RESEALABLE PLASTIC BAG
+ HAMMER
+ 1 OR 2 EGG YOLKS
+ SCISSORS
+ A LARGE CEREAL BOX
+ A VARIETY OF LID SIZES TO TRACE (WE USED FOUR SIZES)
+ RULER
+ PAINTBRUSHES

Soak the bits of chalk in a bowl of water for several minutes to soften them. Put them into a resealable plastic bag, to contain the mess, and pound them lightly with a hammer to break up the chalk into a powdery paste. Mix the chalk paste with the egg yolk until it is the consistency of paint. Be sure to wash your hands thoroughly and clean up any spills promptly and properly. Also, as this paint contains raw egg, you will want to discard any unused paint.

Cut the cereal box into a giant circle using a lid as a template. Measure the distance between your child's eyes. Make the eye holes. Using small lids, create the eye circles around the holes. Use a giant lid to create the lower lip outline. Paint the back of the box—the blank brown side—and embellish.

Modifications for Younger Kids
Instead of using homemade egg paint, have your child finger paint. If you don't have finger paint or are working with a child who puts everything in his/her mouth, add some food coloring to vanilla pudding and use that as "paint."

Modifications for Older Kids
Ask the children to describe their personality or appearance. After they have told you what is distinctive about them, have them try to draw a superhero mask based on the characteristics they described.

Homemade Sidewalk Chalk

The world is our canvas—or at least our driveway! Our kids enjoy tracing their body, creating never-ending hopscotch boards and playing our homemade game of chalk tangle. Some of the best chalk we have used is homemade. Toddlers prefer the chunky sticks. Homemade chalk can be customized for color and color intensity. We think the brighter and more layers of color, the better!

This activity makes sidewalk chalk from scratch. Make extra. Your kids will love to give these sticks to their friends as gifts.

Materials

+ Disposable bowls and spoons or wooden sticks for mixing
+ ½ cup (64 g) cornstarch
+ Water
+ 1 pound (455 g) plaster of paris
+ Multiple colors of tempura paint
+ Empty toilet paper rolls
+ Waxed paper
+ Rubber band(s)

WARNING:
Do not allow your children to touch the plaster with their hands, as it can cause burns. Throw away any unused plaster. Do not rinse out the containers in the house, because the plaster can solidify inside pipes.

Use disposable bowls to mix in and plastic spoons or wooden stir sticks that you can throw away. Because you are using plaster of paris, you do not want to wash anything because it will clog your drain. Small children should not be involved in this first step and we recommend it be done outside.

Mix the cornstarch and water first, and then add the plaster of paris slowly while continuing to stir. It will be the consistency of pancake batter. Once mixed, separate into smaller bowls and add the desired tempura paint color and mix.

Line the empty toilet paper tubes with waxed paper (both inside the tube and underneath where the tube will stand). Spoon the color mixture into the lined toilet paper tubes. If you use a rubber band to bunch a group of rolls, it will make it easier to keep them standing upright.

Let the sticks dry fully, roughly 24 to 48 hours, before removing the paper tubes and heading to the driveway.

Modifications for Younger Kids
Younger kids can direct color coordination and work as an assistant, going and getting things as needed.

Modifications for Older Kids
Have your older kids layer the colors inside each tube to create rainbow sticks. As you draw a line on the sidewalk, it will change colors!

Kick the Can Art

One of the reasons that we are so passionate about kids' activities is that there is no excuse not to play. It doesn't take money or special equipment. Anything can be turned into a game. Kids have known this since the beginning of time. Adults have been known to forget this.

The existence of games like Kick the Can prove this. You play with what you have. The fun in this activity is that you can also create art during your next game.

Materials
(to make one can)

+ SCISSORS
+ SHEETS OF PAPER
+ LARGE, EMPTY, CLEAN COFFEE CAN WITH A LID
+ 2 OR 3 COLORS OF PAINT
+ 3 OR 4 MARBLES OF VARIOUS SIZE
+ TAPE

TIP
To help kids with communication and to keep frustration levels low when kids are not equally matched (say a four-year-old is playing with an eight-year-old), have a "freeze phrase" that younger participants can use once a round that freezes the other players and allows them a chance to get close and kick the can.

Cut the paper to be just a little shorter than the height of the can, so that you can line the entire inside of can with the paper. Squirt paint into the can. Drop the marbles in, then secure the lid with tape.

Kick the can.

It is best to only use two colors of paint, ones that when they mix create a pleasing color—if you use lots of colors, the finished product tends to look more gray or brown, instead of vibrant.

Keep Away
One child is given the can to try to keep it away from a designated home base by kicking it. The other participants attempt to intercept the can and kick it back home. Whenever the can successfully lands on home base, the art project is removed and a new one started. The participant who kicked the can to the goal gets to choose the colors of the new art piece.

Can Soccer
Traditional soccer rules can be modified to accommodate a can (no head butting allowed!) and each time a goal is scored, the art can be reset.

Modifications for Younger Kids
The magical sound of shaking marbles in a tin can may be enough entertainment for the very young. If younger participants want to play, give them special rules that allow them to pick up the can and throw it. Set up an invisible "personal space barrier" of 3 feet (92 cm) so they don't end up in the middle of a kick.

Modifications for Older Kids
If the majority of participants are older, just add one marble to the can. Older kids tend to kick the can more between art resets and fewer marbles will make a more distinctive pattern.

Paper Bag Game Portfolio

I was introduced to the dot game (where you try to complete squares against an opponent) while in kindergarten, when I was on a big yellow school bus en route to a field-trip destination. The time flew by as the games continued. It still seems mysterious to me how one line can cause a chain reaction of squares.

Despite handheld video games and portable video consoles, there is a tactile satisfaction to traditional two-person games battled on paper. This craft creates a safe place to keep and transport a variety of paper games.

Materials
(to make one paper bag book)

+ Scissors
+ 3 or 4 paper lunch bags
+ Hole punch
+ Yarn
+ Copy or construction paper
+ Markers/crayons/paint

TIP
Laminating the paper game inserts and using dry-erase markers can keep the games going and going.

Cut the bottom off the bag to create a paper sleeve. Fold the bag in half. Repeat three to five times for each portfolio.

Stack the bags together, making sure the folded sides are aligned. Hole punch six holes equidistant from one another down the folded side. Secure by lacing and tying yarn through each hole.

Now there are pockets to keep each paper game. Cut paper to fit snuggly in the portfolio and outline the game (or leave the paper blank). Some games we love:

• Tic-tac-toe

• Hangman

• Dots

• Shut the Box

• Finish the Picture

Modifications for Younger Kids
Fill the portfolio with coloring activities and blank paper for doodles.

Modifications for Older Kids
Older kids can choose how to design their portfolio and which games to include. They could also include blank sheets ready for origami, along with the directions for folding.

People Sticks

When I read a book, the characters are vividly brought to life as I see them. I think that is why watching a movie adapted of a favorite book can be so disappointing. Everything doesn't look right!

Kids can create their favorite characters on craft sticks as they see them. Then use these companions as bookmarks, for impromptu puppet shows or for a game of Who Am I?

Materials
+ CRAFT STICKS—1 PER CHARACTER
+ PAINT PENS

TIP
Have kids retell a favorite story, using puppets (or sticks). It will help them with reading comprehension and story sequencing, even if they aren't reading yet.

Decorate the craft sticks, using paint pens to transform it into a favorite book character. It can be as simple or as elaborate as the child imagines.

Modifications for Younger Kids
Cut up a magazine or coloring book and glue the faces or entire bodies onto the sticks.

Modifications for Older Kids
Have them create a complete cast of book characters—even obscure ones—and act out the story, using the upright book as a stage. If they are in a group, have them play a game of Who Am I? with the stick people. Pick a stick from the pile and without looking at it, hold it up to your forehead. The other kids at the table give one clue at a time, describing the character without using the character's name, until the correct character is guessed.

Woven Upcycled Container

Roughly a year and a half ago, we spent some time in Ethiopia, where we adopted our sons. One of my memories of Ethiopia includes a family that wove beautiful hats from wool. This weaving craft is inspired by those industrious kids we met. It is a simple activity using a recycled take-out container and some yarn that can create art and stir memories.

Materials

+ Scissors
+ Square Styrofoam take-out container
+ Various balls of yarn
+ Tape

TIP

This is a great pre-math activity to help preschoolers learn pattern making and develop fine motor skills.

Cut the top off of the take-out container. Wrap one color of yarn around and around the bottom half of the container, leaving ¼ inch (6 mm) or so between strands over the opening. Once you have the desired loom width, tape the end of the yarn to the underside of the makeshift loom. While on the underside, stretch a large piece of tape across all the yarn loops to increase stability on the other side.

Tape around the end of a piece of yarn to create an easily handled "tip." Weave the yarn back and forth over and under the stationary yarn assembled in the loom. Use different colors and different over/under patterns for a unique and colorful creation.

Modifications for Younger Kids

Space the stationary loom strands out further. Consider using a thicker yarn or craft fabric strands. Make sure the color of the yarn used for weaving is different from the stationary loom yarn to make it easier for kids to see the weaving process.

Modifications for Older Kids

Older kids can have the freedom to create an intricate design based on how they use the loom. Finished squares can be sewn together to create scarves, blankets and many other things.

TP Tube Stamping

Kids love to give gifts, but often they are not in a position to do so. That is why we love this activity so much. It gives children the ability to be involved in giving almost any gift by creating the wrapping. It makes them part of the gift team.

Using recycled household items to create a stamp, kids can customize gift bags for recipients in a special way.

Materials
(to make one rolling stamp)

+ FOAM STICKER SHEET OR STICKERS
+ SCISSORS
+ EMPTY TOILET PAPER ROLL
+ PAINT
+ PAPER PLATE
+ PAPER BAG

TIP

Is your gift too large to fit in a bag? Try stamping plain white or brown package paper for custom gift wrap!

Cut the foam sticker sheet or stickers into the desired shape. We cut ours into simple geometric shapes. Peel off the backing and adhere to the toilet paper roll in a pattern. Rows of similar shapes work really well.

Spread paint in a thin layer on a paper plate and roll the toilet paper stamp through it until all the shapes are covered with color. Place the stamp at one end of the bag and roll it down the length. Let dry and then repeat on the other side of the bag.

Modifications for Younger Kids
Use finger paint so younger kids can accent the rolled pattern with some additional hands-on design; the mess can be cleaned up easily.

Modifications for Older Kids
Older kids can create custom tubes with multiple patterns on each tube for stripes of shapes. They can use a paintbrush to apply color to each shape individually for a more precise paint distribution.

Rubber Band Splatter

On a boring afternoon when there is "nothing to do," there is no better way to reverse the melancholy mood than with a messy activity. Kids making a mess are usually smiling! It must have something to do with throwing oneself into a task and feeling the paint fly. Even kids who don't like to get messy have a hard time resisting this activity.

This artistic process uses rubber band snapping to paint a modern art masterpiece (for supervising adults see the tips for containing the mess).

Materials

+ CONSTRUCTION PAPER—CUT TO FIT THE BOTTOM OF THE BOX
+ SMALL BOX OR TUB
+ 3 TO 5 RUBBER BANDS
+ 2 OR 3 COLORS OF TEMPERA PAINT
+ PAINTBRUSH

TIPS

This activity should be done with kids wearing old clothes. If creating art inside, consider using a drop cloth or old towels or use it as a pre-bath activity in the tub.

If you don't want a mess at all, remove the idea of paint and let the kids create a rubber band instrument. They will enjoy the noises it makes.

Place a piece of paper in the bottom of your box. Stretch the rubber bands across the top of the box. Paint the rubber bands with a variety of colors.

Pull on the bands to watch the paint splatter onto the paper below.

Modifications for Younger Kids

For smaller children, use edible paint. Kids who are prone to putting their fingers into their mouth can enjoy the activity, too.

Modifications for Older Kids

Older kids can work toward a more predictable end result through organized color coordination and rubber band snapping.

Shake-It-Up Ink

I love a new set of markers. The colors are so bright and the lines they create are crisp. The problem with markers is that over time, they lose their marker*ness.* Opening up a marker that doesn't work is a big disappointment. This activity uses those underachieving markers to create ink that gives them a leading role in a splotch art masterpiece.

Materials

+ EMPTY, CLEAN SMALL GLASS JARS WITH LIDS
+ OLD DRIED-OUT MARKERS—5 OR SO FOR EACH COLOR
+ BOTTLE OF RUBBING ALCOHOL
+ KITCHEN PAN
+ MULTIPLE SYRINGES OR MEDICINE DROPPERS
+ PAPER

Use a separate glass jars for each color you want to create. Open up the old markers and place the colorful core in the jar for that desired color. When all the marker cores are distributed, pour rubbing alcohol over them with enough liquid to cover.

Place the lids on the jars and let the kids shake the odd concoction. Let the jars sit overnight to allow the ink to fully form.

Fill a kitchen pan with water and slide a piece of paper through it to dampen the page. Use the water for color changes and cleanup. Then fill a syringe or medicine dropper with the newly formed ink and drop onto the damp paper.

Watch how the colorful drops start small and seep out into colorful bursts.

Modifications for Younger Kids

Children who have difficulty controlling a syringe or medicine dropper can be given a filled ear bulb, which uses more gross vs. fine motor coordination.

Modifications for Older Kids

Have older kids experiment with creating new colors by combining marker core colors. They can also try this project on dry paper to see what a difference the dampness can make.

TIPS

Using a medicine dropper can help develope fine motor skills, which can help strengthen little hands for tasks like writing and picking up small objects. This can help prewriters more easily control their pencil grasp, and strength in older kids can translate into better coordination.

Looking to give a fun and unique gift? Replace the paper with ceramic tiles and watch your kids create one-of-a-kind coasters for friends and family. Glue felt to the back of the tiles.

Shrinking Cup Flower Sculptures

While growing up, I was mesmerized by Shrinky Dinks. Because they were out of my allowance range, it was a rare occurrence to be able to draw something on a thin plastic sheet and then bake it into a magically appearing keychain. The whole process was awesome.

These flower sculptures use a similar concept to transform plain clear plastic cups into colorful art. The good news is that the allowance can stay in the jar!

Materials

+ CLEAR PLASTIC CUPS
+ COLORFUL PERMANENT MARKERS
+ SCISSORS
+ BAKING SHEET AND OVEN (USE WITH ADULT SUPERVISION)

Decorate the clear plastic cups with various colors and patterns. Use scissors to cut slits every inch (2.5 cm) or so around the rim of the cups, leaving the bottom of the cups intact.

Place the colorful cups on a baking sheet. Place in an oven at 350°F (180°C or gas mark 4) for a minute. Watch carefully so as not to overmelt.

Let the flower cool before touching.

Try using a deeper clear plastic cup and leaving the bottom two-thirds unslit, to create a usable vase.

Modifications for Younger Kids
Younger kids can help decorate and design flowers, while saving the cutting and baking for adults.

Modifications for Older Kids
Older kids can plan what the finished project will look like through several trials of flower making. Petals could be shaped more specifically with scissors and colors coordinated to imitate real flowers.

Soap Surprises

Cracker Jack and cereal packagers knew the secret to captivating a kid audience. Promise a secret treat buried in the box and watch kids unearth the treasure at the expense of perfectly good food. In my house there is a rule that the prize cannot be reached for. It has to fall out on its own. In some cases, this caused a week of eating cereal with no reward. It can be brutal.

It isn't that the actual treat is so amazing. It is the waiting. It is the hunt. This soap activity exploits the hunt into wash time. Hide secret treasures in soap that can only be revealed through washing. It is a win-win for both kids and parents.

Materials
(to make five Soap Surprises)

+ Kitchen grater
+ 2 soap bars
+ 2 bowls
+ Blue or other food coloring
+ Microwave-safe bowl
+ Microwave
+ Spoon
+ Small, inexpensive treasures

Using a cheese grater on the largest hole size, grate the soap into one bowl. In a second bowl, change the color of half of the batch with your desired color of food coloring. Place a handful each of the colored gratings and the plain gratings in the microwave-safe bowl. Add a tablespoon (14 ml) or so of water and microwave at full power for 10 seconds. Remove from the oven and stir. If the soap is a moldable texture, then proceed to the next step. If not, add a bit more water and repeat the microwaving process.

Mold the soap around a treasure, making sure to cover all its edges. Create a soap ball or bar with your hands. Let the ball set overnight before use.

Modifications for Younger Kids
Give your kids a spoon. Young children love to stir, and stir and stir. You can't over- or undermix your soap shavings. Do this on your kitchen floor and some of the bits are guaranteed to fall on the floor. Let your tots mop up the floor in their socks when you are finished.

Modifications for Older Kids
Have older kids try to push the soap into large cookie cutters for molding at the end. Create a soap bath set for a sibling or friend as a gift.

TIP
Add a science experiment to your soap-making activity. Watch water and air molecules literally expand by leaving Ivory soap (has to be Ivory soap) in the microwave. Watch the soap grow and expand as the air inside the soap expands.

Solar Oven Crayon Art

Sometime this summer, the kids are going to say it is too hot to play outside. My kids have been known to say this on a breezy April Texas day, causing my automatic lecture about how an additional 20°F (5.6°C) and more is in store over the next few months and they should enjoy this perfect weather.

This activity is one to save for when you hear the complaint. Showing kids how to harness the sun for their enjoyment is much more effective than my automatic lecture.

Materials

+ Shoe box
+ Tinfoil
+ Old crayons
+ Scraps of thick cardboard

Line the box with tinfoil and set it in the sun. Send the kids on an expedition.

Peel off the crayon wrappers and get the colors ready for use. Place the crayon bits on the cardboard. Place the cardboard in the solar box. As the crayons melt, they will seep into the cardboard for an interesting puddle effect.

Depending on the weather, the crayon bits should melt within 30 minutes. If the sun is not strong enough to melt the crayon bits, due to the time of year or climate in your area, you can transfer this activity to your kitchen oven. Line a cookie sheet to avoid any waxy spills. Set the oven temperature at 170°F (77°C, or gas mark less than ¼).

Modifications for Younger Kids

Keep in mind that the melting crayon bits are hot, and from experience we can warn you: melted crayon wax stains everything. Plan accordingly.

Modifications for Older Kids

Older kids could modify the oven design, try it at different times of day and chart how long it takes to melt the crayon bits. Do different colors melt at faster rates than others?

Story Layers

Story sequencing is key to communication. Kids learn this innately through telling their own stories, creating flip books and adding layers to their story as in this activity. We use clear plastic lids upcycled from take-out containers to create a blank canvas to tell a multidimensional story.

Materials

+ Multiple clear plastic containers or lids
+ Scissors
+ Tape or glue
+ Craft sticks
+ Blank construction or copy paper for theater background
+ Permanent marker

If using the clear clamshell-type takeout container, cut through the lid attachment so there are two separate pieces. Create a group of similarly sized clear canvases for artwork.

Show the kids how they will be able to layer the elements on top of one another so each lid only needs to show part of the story.

Start with the setting. Have kids draw what the surroundings of the story look like on the first clear lid.

Then on the next lid, have them add a character and any details surrounding that character. The next lid can introduce another character and story parts that the character might change. Another lid can wrap up the story with a conclusion or solution to the characters' problems.

Tape or glue craft sticks to the bottom of each of the clear plastic lids and number them.

Set up a theater with a plain paper background. Have the child start telling his/her story with the first layer and then continue the story by adding the other layers one by one.

Challenge kids to pick up a friend's or sibling's story and come up with a different story, using the same sequence of scenes.

Modifications for Younger Kids

Have kids tell you a story that you help them draw. When they are telling the story, ask questions to encourage more thought and detail.

Modifications for Older Kids

Have older kids create longer stories with more than one series of scenes. They could also create an additional layer by decorating the backdrop to complement their unique story.

This activity helps older kids learn story sequencing, but also reinforces scale and space when drawing. The planning required for placing a story element to be seen through several scenes as the story continues is a challenge even for older children.

Tinfoil Relief

My kids' first exposure to the art concept of relief, where part of the picture is raised from the background, was with pencil rubbings at church. One of my standard quiet activities is to place the church bulletin over the embossed front cover of the songbook and show them how a pencil can be used to transfer the word *hymnal* to the paper.

This art project uses this common household item for a sunk-relief masterpiece. Using a bit of yarn and some paint, your child can transform a piece of tinfoil into something really, really cool.

Materials

+ STICKY YARN (OR YARN AND GLUE)
+ PIECE OF CARDBOARD
+ TINFOIL
+ MASKING TAPE
+ SPRAY PAINT
+ SCRUBBING PAD (AS FOR DISHES)

TIP

Do you have leftover tinfoil? Consider watching your tots create a ball with it. They will enjoy feeling the foil crinkle as they form the ball.

Create shapes with the sticky yarn on the cardboard. We created geometric shapes. The possibilities are endless.

After you have the yarn design laid out, press the yarn down lightly to make sure it won't move.

Cover your yarn with the foil. Tape the foil down to the back of the cardboard.

Rub the foil to make the yarn "bump," or become raised.

Go outside and spray paint the foil-covered cardboard.

Let the paint fully dry before lightly buffing the yarn relief with the dish scrubber. Buffing will remove the paint, showing the design of the yarn through the paint.

Modifications for Younger Kids
Let younger kids help with all the steps, excluding the spray painting, or skip the spray paint altogether.

Modifications for Older Kids
Encourage older kids to create a series of related relief works to display together.

Water Bottle Bangles

I once made a craft that I had seen on a TV DIY show. It required a trip to the local craft supply store for materials. When it was completed, I realized it had taken a full day and the supplies cost three times what it was worth. On top of that, I wasn't skilled at the craft and my final project didn't quite look right. The whole thing was a mess!

That is one of the things that inspired crafts like this DIY bracelet. It requires no trip to the local craft store for materials and the final project will look great no matter the skill level of the crafter.

Materials
(to make two or three bangles)

+ EMPTY WATER BOTTLE
+ COLORFUL PERMANENT MARKERS
+ SCISSORS

TIP

Have boys who don't want to wear bracelets? Have them make a set in two different colors and then use them for a ring toss game.

Decorate the empty water bottle with markers. You can use the indented rings in many commercial water bottles to create color stripes and blocks. Cut the water bottle into 1½- to 3-inch (4 to 7.5 cm) -wide rings.

Modifications for Younger Kids
If little arms are too small for wearing bracelets, this project makes the perfect size ring toy. Check scissors-cut areas for any sharp or rough edges and smooth with sandpaper or cover with a durable tape.

Modifications for Older Kids
Kids can design their own bracelets of different widths and decorations for a planned stacked fashion statement.

(three)

GAMES

There is a game in nearly everything. It isn't about the rules or who wins. They are a great way to learn skills like teamwork, strategy, conflict, decision making, cause and effect, problems, solutions and payoffs in a low-stakes situation. Games are just fun!

Holly's Pick: It is hard for me to pick just one game as a favorite. The ones that we play the most at home are Funnel Golf Toss (page 122) and Family Four Square (page 112). Both games are highly competitive, inspire "house rules" and generally end in friendly trash-talking.

Rachel's Pick: Our boys were amazed at how far the Egg Carton Glider Sails (page 121)! It is, by far, their favorite "airplane"—easy to make and encourages your kids to eat eggs so they can use the carton to fly.

Over & Under Obstacle Course

Creating an indoor obstacle course is an easy way to get kids moving inside. It works great on a rainy, too cold or too hot day to work out the wiggles. Course design is only limited by the obstacle potential seen in furniture and objects around the house. Starting with something simple like this over and under obstacle course can inspire creative station additions to make the obstacle course uniquely your own.

- -

Materials

+ 3 X 5-INCH (7.5 X 12.5 CM) CARDS
+ MARKER
+ CHAIRS/STOOLS/OTTOMANS
+ TAPE

TIP

Create homemade medals and a three-tier award stand for an indoor Olympic ceremony based on the results of the over and under obstacle competition.

On each 3 x 5-inch (7.5 x 12.5 cm) card, have a child draw an arrow. You will need an arrow for each of the chair obstacles on your course.

Set up chairs, stools and ottomans, leaving space between them, throughout a room or hallway. Your course can be limited to one room or spread out throughout the house. On each piece of furniture, tape an arrow that indicates whether that obstacle needs to be negotiated by going over or under it. You can also use arrows to mark the course and direct kids around things.

Set start and finish lines.

Kids will love running the course just by following the arrows, but if you want to add a little competition, then time them on a stopwatch and have them try to beat their time on each run through.

Modifications for Younger Kids

Shorten the course for the youngest participants and make an under-only path.

Modifications for Older Kids

Let older kids design the course within the parameters of what furniture is course-worthy. The last time we did this at our house, the kids had a course with twenty-two stations! Have them chart their times for each trial.

Balloon Bean Bags

When I was in sixth grade, I learned to juggle. It wasn't something that would entertain others in a coordinated way. It was something that I spent hours mastering in the large semifinished basement at home.

These bean bags are super easy to make—perfect for little hands and for aspiring jugglers.

- -

Materials

+ A ⅓ cup (80 ml) measuring cup
+ Rice, wheat berries, sand or flour
+ Balloons
+ Funnel

TIP

Help your kids develop hand strength. Use flour as the balloon filler and it becomes a "stress ball." These also make great "hot potatoes" for an impromptu game.

We measured precisely ⅓ cup (80 ml) of balloon "filler." We wanted every balloon bag to weigh the same amount. Secure the balloon to the bottom of a funnel and pour your measured amount into the funnel and fill up the balloon. Tie the balloons.

Use a bean bag to toss back and forth among all participants. Once one bag is in play, add another. It is fun to watch how intently kids will pay attention trying to predict when the bean bag is headed in their direction.

Add a pattern to the toss—two people throw to each other at the same time or each person tosses to the person on the left. Have someone lead the directions and change the pattern.

This is also a great solo play activity. Starting with one bag, toss it into the air and catch it, eventually working toward juggling with three bags . . . or more!

Modifications for Younger Kids
Instead of making bags that weigh the same amounts, consider making each bag different. Have younger children explore the different textures of the various fillers, and organize them by weight or "feeling."

Modifications for Older Kids
When creating the bean bags, have older kids try to make three bags exactly the same weight. Weigh them on a scale when you are finished. See whether they are the same and make adjustments to the filling as needed. Use the three matched bags to learn to juggle.

Bathtime Memory Game

The game of Memory is a staple of childhood because it is one of the few games where adults and kids are competitive equals. It was one of the first games that I beat my dad in. As a parent now, I can see that he likely didn't throw the game. Children are good at remembering and they delight in victory!

This Memory game is a solo bath version. It is created with sponge tiles that can be decorated in the theme of the child's choice.

Materials
+ 6 OR MORE SPONGES
+ SCISSORS
+ PERMANENT MARKER

TIP
Are your sponges starting to smell "off"? You can kill the bacteria in them by heating a wet sponge in the microwave for 15 seconds or so. The heat will kill the bacteria, increasing the life of the sponge.

Cut the sponges into uniform rectangles. The size and shape doesn't matter as long as they are all the same. Pair the pieces and with a permanent marker create the exact same pattern on one side of each paired piece.

When the sponge tiles are moist, they will stick to the wall of most bathtub surfaces. Place the tiles pattern side down in randomly selected rows. Kids play by turning over two tiles each turn, trying to find the matching pair.

Modifications for Younger Kids
Larger and fewer sponge tiles work best and make fabulous bath toys even if the child isn't in the mood for playing a game.

Modifications for Older Kids
Use the pairs to match upper- and lowercase letters, or numbers and the number words. Place sight words on the tiles for a fun reading practice.

Beach Ball Carry

Group problem solving happens within a family daily. It is something that we might not think about, but figuring out how to juggle food preferences, sleeping schedules, sporting schedules, laundry, homework and family fun within the family's available time is a big task. Creating games around working as a group can help even the family's smallest members start creatively finding ways to work together for a common goal.

This activity is a simple way to team build among a group of children or a family unit. A sheet and a ball can be the catalyst for a group solution.

Materials
(for two or more children)

+ BEDSHEET
+ LARGE BEACH BALL

Use the sheet to carry the ball to a specified destination. This can be a simple start and finish line or obstacles can be placed in the way to negotiate around, under and over, depending on the age of your participants. If the group drops the ball on the ground during the process, they start back at the beginning.

Modifications for Younger Kids

- Make the ball smaller. Tennis balls also work. You can have your children do an obstacle course where they have to drop multiple balls into different pockets.

- Allow the kids to use two hands to hold the sheet.

- If they are too young to enjoy following directions, maybe just make the only rule that the ball cannot touch the ground and watch them bounce the ball in the air, trying to catch it together.

Modifications for Older Kids

- Use a small sheet and a big ball. Tell them they are not allowed to touch the ball once placed on the sheet.

- Make them only use one hand and try to figure out ways to hold the sheet and keep the ball on it.

- Add speed. Have your children see how fast they can complete their mission.

- Change the height. Make the place where they have to deposit the ball up high, like on top of an outdoor toy or bush. They have to problem solve to find a way to get the ball up there.

- Help your kids become effective communicators. Blindfold a child and ask a partner to help him/her complete the task by relying on communication.

Garden Game Boards

We are happiest when we get a daily dose of the outdoors. It is not unusual for us to be outside for the majority of a day. While the younger kids enjoy just digging in the dirt and collecting leaves, the older kids prefer something more structured.

If your kids love being outside, but are also social and want to be "doing" something, this might be the perfect project for you. Your kids can scheme up and recreate their favorite games and you can use them over and over!

Materials

+ SMALL PIZZA BOX
+ WAXED PAPER
+ QUICK-SET CEMENT
+ POWDERED CHALK OR ACRYLIC PAINT TO DYE THE CEMENT
+ DISPOSABLE PLASTIC KNIFE

Suggested items or ways to create your game boards. Use all or just some of the ideas.

+ COINS, SHELLS, MARBLES, ROCKS, BEADS
+ PAINT
+ NAILS

Line your pizza box with waxed paper. Mix the cement according to the instructions provided by the manufacturer. Add crushed chalk or acrylic paint to the cement to dye it if you want a colorful board. Carefully fill the box with the cement. After the cement has started to "gel," smooth the top of the cement with the plastic knife to help even out the lumps. Add embellishment items from the above list to create your game board! You will want to put your embellished board somewhere dry to set for 24 hours before removing the box and the paper backing.

Game Board Ideas

- **GeoBoard:** Add nails in increments staggered around the board. To play, grab a handful of rubber bands and stretch them around the nails to create different shapes.

- **Tic-Tac-Toe Board:** Use old pencils or pens to create the "grid" for the tic-tac-toe board. Use two different types of leaves from your yard as the game pieces for this classic!

- **Connect the Dots:** Evenly place marbles along the top of your board, in a grid pattern. To play, use chalk or blades of grass to connect the dots. You can play multiple games with this board. You can create mazes, you can try to see who can close the most "boxes," you can draw a design going from "dot to dot," and so forth.

Modifications for Younger Kids

Just make a smooth surface and use it as a chalkboard. This is especially great to have if you don't like having your kids decorate all over the patio—give them a "creative space."

Modifications for Older Kids

Ask your kids to create a new game: maybe mix two of their favorite games together and have them create a set of rules to follow so as to play their new game.

Family Four Square

The simple game of Four Square was a staple of my childhood. It was a game that I played with classmates before school on stretches of bumpy asphalt with stick and stone boundary markers.

I hadn't thought about the game until nearly a year ago, when my oldest son took me outside to teach me a game they play at school all the time. It was fun to see the look on his face when I showed him that Four Square isn't a skill you lose with time.

This is a team adaptation of the traditional game where the team competes against itself in pattern play to set a new family record.

Materials

+ Sidewalk chalk (page 77) or painter's tape
+ Driveway
+ Rubber ball

TIP

This is a great game to play with grandparents as long as they are given special rules according to their skill level, just like the younger players! At our house, Grandma is always given two bounces.

Use chalk or tape to measure out a square with a width of approximately 20 feet (about 6 m). Divide the large square into four equal squares of 10 feet (about 3 m) each.

Number the squares 1 through 4, with special marks in the fourth square.

Each player stands in one of the squares. Extra players form a line at the outside boundary of square 1.

The player in square 4 serves the ball by bouncing it and hitting it gently in an underhand, open palm motion to another square. The receiving player allows the ball to bounce one time and then hits it underhand and open palm to the next player's square in the sequence.

The object of the game is for each player to hit the ball to the next player in a way that they can complete the action, trying to keep their streak of no double bounces or out of bounds hits, going through as many rounds as possible. Once a streak is broken, all players rotate (1 goes to 2; 2 to 3; and so on, with the 4 starting at square 1 or the end of the square 1 line) and start another streak.

Each of the patterns is played for one round and it is up to the 4 square server to change the pattern when the ball arrives back to him. If the sequence is broken, then the next server starts at the first pattern again.

• Clockwise

• Counterclockwise

• Crisscross

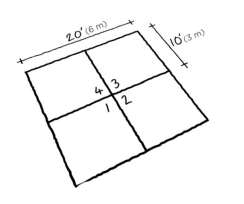

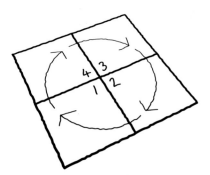

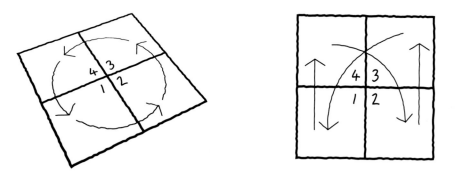

The sequence repeats until broken, with the team keeping track of how many rounds they successfully complete.

Modifications for Younger Kids

Younger kids will do better with a lighter, larger ball. Depending on their age/skill, implementing special rules like two bounces or rolls only to their square can make them an important part of the team.

Modifications for Older Kids

Older kids can take turns calling the plays—reminding everyone of the direction of play or which pattern is next in line. Give them the ability to choose a fourth pattern to the sequence, such as:

- Crisscross rolls only

- Big bounces left

- Double bounces right

Catapult Competition

Weapons are a big deal at our house. It wasn't my kids' environment that created this obsession; it is just how they are! Early on we didn't have any toy weapons for play, which led to my children constructing them.

I thought it might be best to harness this weapon creativity for good vs. evil, and this catapult competition is the result of this maternal guidance.

Kids can use things around the house to construct a catapult and then compete for catapult dominance bragging rights.

Materials
(to make one catapult)

+ SCISSORS
+ 14 WIDE CRAFT STICKS
+ 7 RUBBER BANDS
+ PLASTIC SPOON
+ PAINTER'S TAPE
+ TAPE MEASURE
+ PING-PONG BALLS OR OTHER PROJECTILES LIKE POM-POMS, COTTON BALLS, ETC.

Start by snipping 2 inches (5 cm) off each end of one craft stick, using scissors. Stack nine craft sticks, then center the shorter craft stick on top and then add two more craft sticks. Secure that bundle with two rubber bands placed about one-third of the way in from each end. The shortened stick will be the third stick from the top.

Center a plastic spoon upright against the sides of the craft stick stack. Use a rubber band on each side to wrap it crisscross to keep it in place. Take a third rubber band and loop it so that the top and bottom are around the front of the spoon above and below the craft stick bundle, and the back transverses the back of the bundle.

Add two more craft sticks perpendicular to the stack by inserting them into the space created by the shortened craft stick on each side. Add two more rubber bands—one on each end—to keep the perpendicular sticks in place.

Make a starting line at one end of the play area out of painter's tape. This is where the catapults will be positioned. Stretch the tape measure out at a perpendicular angle from the starting line.

Take turns shooting the projectiles from the catapult. With a small piece of painter's tape that has been labeled with the shooter's initials, mark the landing places. Measure the flight distance and record on a scoreboard.

The player with the highest distance average is declared the winner.

TIP

This activity is great for a group. Precut the one shortened stick and make up a bag for each child that has all the catapult pieces. Build them together and then have a catapult distance battle.

Modification for Younger Kids

One of the frustrating things about a homemade catapult is that it might take a little more coordination to keep the projectile in the spoon while pulling it back than the child can handle. Add a small loop of painter's tape to lightly hold the projectile in the spoon. The catapult action will overcome this slight resistance and allow a younger child to play along.

Modifications for Older Kids

Older kids can create multiple models based on trial and error to design the ultimate catapult for battle. They can test the craft stick catapults against ones that they make with other building toys you may have, like LEGO blocks, Tinker Toys and Erector sets.

Chalk Tangle

Recess was the highlight of my day. There were all the favorite games like Four Square, Dodgeball, Red Rover and Tetherball. And then there were the rainy days when my teacher would reach for the spinner card and pull out the Twister mat, making rainy-day recess as fun as any other day.

There is no reason to wait for rain. This outdoor Twister-inspired activity uses sidewalk chalk and homemade dice to take the fun outside.

- -

Materials
+ AT LEAST 6 COLORS OF SIDEWALK CHALK (PAGE 77)
+ DICE

TIP
Dip your chalk into water before drawing with it on the sidewalk; the colors will be brighter this way.

With sidewalk chalk create a grid six squares across and six squares down. Randomly color in the squares with six different chalk colors, making six squares of each color.

With one of the dice, color each side of the die a different color with chalk. Participants all start standing in the color of their choice. The die roller will call out a body part and then roll the die to determine which color will receive that body part. Participants scramble to comply with the instructions without falling over.

Modifications for Younger Kids
Make the shapes smaller and closer together. Instead of reaching and staying still during the game, smaller participants can try to jump to the color called.

This is a great activity for those kids learning right and left! It will also help your children develop stronger core muscles as they balance on all fours. If you don't have six colors of sidewalk chalk, try using differently shaped flat objects from around the house (a book, a lid, etc.). Have your children land on a square, triangle, circle, diamond, rectangle or hexagon.

Modifications for Older Kids
Create a second die that has body parts listed: right arm, left arm, right leg, left leg, head and so on. Roll both dice to play the game. The kids have to match both the color and the body part.

Craft Stick Domino Game

My family is filled with game players. Saturday night is the designated game night. We have hours of competition over Monopoly, Rook, Clue and other games. One game that all of the members of our family love, from preschooler to grandparent, is Dominoes. This activity creates domino tiles out of craft sticks for a simplified game that doesn't need to be saved for game night.

Materials

+ 20 TO 30 MINI CRAFT STICKS (WE USED ICE CREAM STICKS)
+ MARKERS OR PAINT PENS

Break out the markers! This is a fun activity for your kids. Your child gets to decorate two ends of two sticks. Throw them back into the pile and grab another two sticks to decorate. Continue until every stick has had artwork added to both ends of the sticks.

For young children, it can be hard to create two identical images. If your children are too young to understand the concept of "copying" their artworks, maybe they can make the original and you can copy the pattern that they created on one stick—making the "match."

Patterns can be anything under the sun (including the sun) and don't have to be limited to pictures or symbols. Use letters, numbers and words, too.

The number of sticks you use is up to you. The more you have, the bigger the game. We suggest starting with at least twenty.

Modifications for Younger Kids

Play a game of I Spy collaboratively with your younger preschoolers. With all the patterns facing upright, pick up one stick and ask the kids to find the partner. Match them together and model how to play dominoes as you pick new patterns.

Modifications for Older Kids

Older kids might appreciate more structure. As you create patterns, line them up in a train of matching ends to ensure that you have just one set of matching ends and that they are arranged in a way that the train is continuous when and the caboose matches the engine to complete a circle.

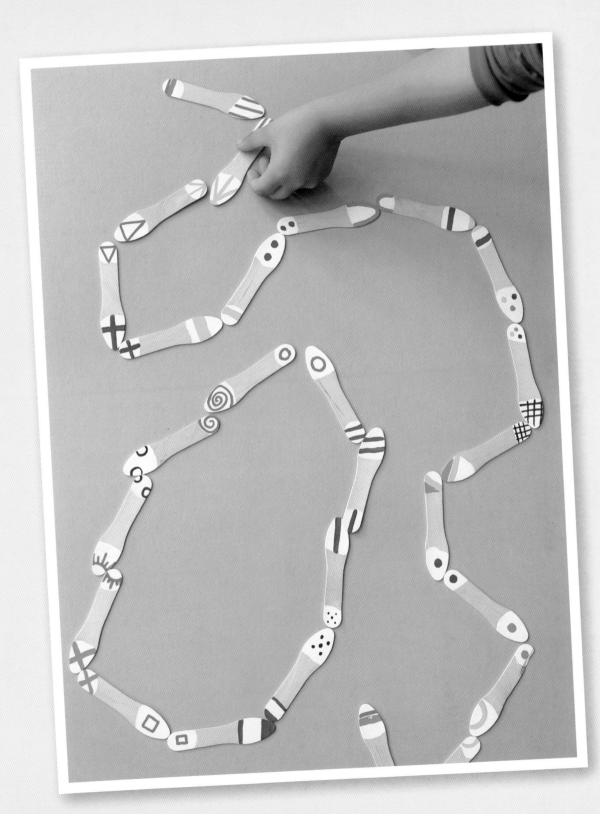

Egg Carton Glider Target Throw

Many airplane kits that we have purchased through the years don't last too long. An inevitable crash takes them out of commission within a few minutes of assembly. Thankfully, this DIY kit uses things found around the house and is sturdier for play, so it doesn't have to be banished to a high shelf to keep it intact. In fact, make a few gliders to use in this target throwing game.

Materials
(to make one glider)

+ Pencil/marker
+ Styrofoam egg carton—an 18-count carton works best, but a dozen also functions
+ Scissors
+ Colorful tape (optional)
+ Heavy-duty binder clip
+ Hula hoop

Using a pencil or marker, sketch your glider design on the Styrofoam egg carton, creating the largest wing span possible (see example). Cut along the lines you created.

Decorate the glider with colorful tape and markers. Affix a binder clip to the front to add weight and stability to the glider.

One player is in charge of moving the target (vertically held hula hoop) and the others throw the planes toward the target. The object is to work together to get the planes to fly smoothly through the hula hoop.

Modifications for Younger Kids

Younger kids will need help with the sketching and cutting of the glider. They can direct the tape placement and decorate with markers. If there are babies in the family, give them the leftover (clean) egg carton pieces to explore and destroy under supervision.

Modifications for Older Kids

Older kids can create a fleet of airplanes, experimenting with different shapes, styles and balances, honing a design that works the best for reaching a target. For older kids who have a younger sibling, increase their challenge by placing the youngest child in charge of the goal. You may end up throwing to a very moving target!

Funnel Golf Toss

Funnel Golf Toss is a modified version of a game my brother and I used to play on the golf course when we accompanied my dad for eighteen (very long) holes of golf. This version doesn't require clubs or acres of grass. It can be set up in the space that you have outdoors or taken to the park to mimic the acres available at the golf course.

Materials

+ CONSTRUCTION PAPER
+ SCISSORS
+ MARKERS
+ 5 TO 18 PLASTIC FUNNELS (ONE FOR EACH HOLE)
+ SKEWER STICKS
+ TAPE
+ SMALL BALL LIKE PING-PONG BALL, GOLF BALL OR EVEN A SMALL BOUNCY BALL

TIP

A discount store can be a treasure trove of inexpensive funnels. Look for nested sets. The smaller funnels can be used alongside the larger ones, for older, more experienced opponents.

Cut the construction paper into triangular flags. Number your flags starting with 1. Make one for each funnel that you have. Attach the flags to skewer sticks with tape.

Push the small end of the plastic funnel into the ground to create a golf "hole." The top of the funnel doesn't need to be flush with the ground because this game doesn't include putting. Place a numbered flag next to each hole. Designate a starting place a distance from flag 1.

We use rules similar to those for the game of golf. Players have to pick up their ball where it lays and not take any steps before throwing. Once a hole is completed, a radius of 3 feet (92 cm) around that hole is the "tee box" for the next hole.

Each throw counts as a stroke and the player with the lowest score at the end of the game wins.

Modifications for Younger Kids

A heavier ball like a golf ball is easier to control and throw. Very small children can be spotted the advantage of taking steps between throws.

Modifications for Older Kids

A lighter ball like a Ping-Pong ball can help level the playing field when playing with younger children. It can't be thrown as far and is harder to land in the funnel hole without bouncing out.

Great Airplane Race

Making paper airplanes is one of our go-to boredom busters because we always have the materials on hand. This activity uses cereal boxes to make larger aircraft, creating mega-size folded airplanes that are perfect for a race as large as their size.

Materials

+ CLEAN, EMPTY CEREAL BOX
+ SCISSORS
+ TAPE
+ PIECE OF ROPE (OPTIONAL)

TIP

If you are using this primarily for outside play, consider weatherizing it by spray painting the plane and adding a traditional paper clip to the nose for flight durability.

Open up the empty cereal box, creating one large piece of cardboard. Cut off the glued tabs as well as any flaps so you are left with a large rectangle.

Fold the box into a traditional paper airplane. Tape the airplane together across the wings to secure it.

Create a finish line out of tape or rope placed on the ground. Each player throws his plane toward the goal. If the plane does not cross the finish line in the first throw, then he walks to where the plane landed and without taking an additional step, throws again, keeping track of how many throws it takes to get to the end.

Modifications for Younger Kids

Younger kids will need some help creating the plane. The stiff cardboard is challenging for little hands. They could use stickers to create a unique design. Use the counting of the throws to reinforce number skills.

Modifications for Older Kids

Older kids can get creative with plane design. They can experiment with new folds and weights and check the results until they find a way to fly further in one throw.

Homemade Building Block Puzzle

This homemade puzzle project uses the toys your kids already have and love in a new way. A handful of favorite blocks and a printer can start a new learning process that your kids will embrace. Depending on their age, you can modify it to be simple or have them create a complex set of building instructions.

Materials
+ BUILDING BLOCKS
+ PAPER OR CARDSTOCK
+ COPIER
+ LAMINATION (OPTIONAL)

Lay the blocks on the copier bed and cover with a white piece of paper or cardstock. The blocks can create a picture or pattern or just be arranged randomly.

Make a color copy of the blocks.

Mix up the pieces used for the original creation with some additional pieces. Have the child use the copy as a template to position the piece on top to recreate the structure.

Modifications for Younger Kids
Use large blocks and less assembly for the template picture as a simple shape-sorter activity.

Modifications for Older Kids
Older kids can make color copies of various steps required to make a more complicated structure. Instead of simple blocks, they could use building sets to create their own assembly guide.

Paper Plate Reversi

One of our favorite family vacation locations has life-size board games situated throughout the village. You can stop and play a very large set of Chess, Scrabble, Jenga and Connect Four, among some others. The games are the biggest attractions despite other (and more expensive) things to do.

We didn't just want that experience on vacation, so we came home and made our own large version of Othello, which we call Reversi. It can be played indoors and packed up to play another day.

Materials

+ Glue (or double-sided tape)
+ 36 paper or plastic plates in two different colors
+ Masking tape

Glue two plates together so that each side is a different color, creating eighteen game pieces. Use tape to create a 6 x 6 square grid on the floor.

Start with four game pieces in the middle four spaces—two of one color and two alternating. Then the players take turns placing their color piece on the other side of an opponent's piece. Once a color piece is surrounded on two sides by another color, it can be flipped. The object of the game is to flip as many of your opponent's pieces as possible. The game ends when all the spaces are filled. The person with the most color showing, wins.

Modifications for Younger Kids

A big grid on the floor and colorful pieces don't have to have real rules! Let kids create stacks of color or make simple art in the grid. Practicing colors and counting while playing can enforce basic skills.

Modifications for Older Kids

This is a fun game for kids of all ages and something that kids can be competitive with adults. Add more rows to make the game more complicated for older kids. Let your space be your guide and create a massive board with additional pieces for a really, really big game. You can also play the game with a stopwatch and anyone taking more than 5 seconds forfeits that turn.

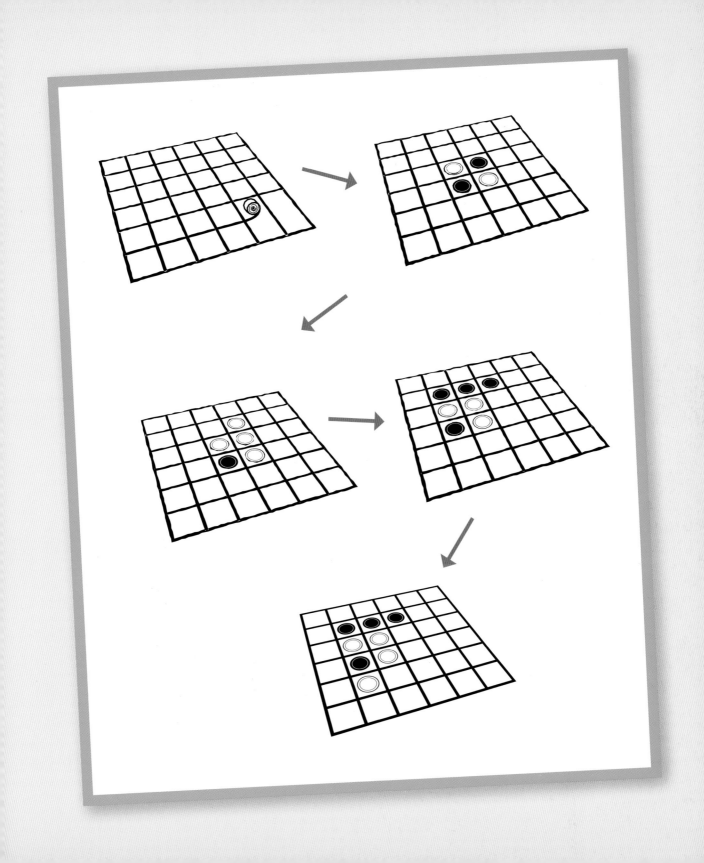

Human Knot

Some kids are drawn to knots. They have an uncanny way of being able to tie and untie them. My relative Jeannette is like that. She has always been the go-to person for untangling just about anything. She is the one you would want to take with you on a kite flying expedition.

This activity was inspired in part by her love of knots. Use group participants' limbs wrapped together to create a life-size puzzle that requires giggles to solve.

- -

Five or more kiddos works well; fewer than ten is best. Have the kids group together (not orderly, it works best if this "hand grab" is chaotic). Have the children raise their left hands, and have them grab one of the raised hands (not their own). Then repeat with their right hands. Everyone should now be bunched up together, holding hands with two other people. They are one giant human knot!

Without letting go of each other's hands, the kids need to figure out how to unknot the human pretzel that they formed. They will need to climb under and over each other in order to detangle the knot. In the end, the hands should make a giant circle.

Modifications for Younger Kids
Creating a human knot with fewer participants can make it easier to solve. Have one of the kids not in the knot give the participants directions to help them solve the problem.

Modifications for Older Kids
Watch them struggle. This can be a fun group activity with several groups of the same number of kids competing against each other to unknot the quickest.

Recycled Bottle Cup Catch

So many products these days have really fun bottles that can be upcycled into really cool toys. This activity was inspired by my morning coffee habit. I always have refrigerated creamer and the bottles have a unique shape. The product labels are shrink-wrapped, which means that they are easily removed to find a blank canvas for all sorts of crafty goodness.

A string, a bottle and a Ping-Pong ball make a fun cup catch game that you can play by yourself or with a partner.

Materials
(to make one cup catch)

+ Empty plastic bottle
+ Serrated knife
+ Paint (optional)
+ Small ball—I used a Ping-Pong ball
+ Screw eye hook
+ Glue (optional)
+ String

Remove any labels from the empty plastic bottle and then cut off the bottom of the bottle with a serrated knife. Many plastic bottles have indented rings that work great as a cutting guide.

I spray painted the bottles at this point, but leaving it plain works great, too.

For the Solo Game
Poke a small hole in the Ping-Pong ball and then screw in the hook. If it seems loose, then unscrew the hook and add a little glue to the screw threads before reinserting.

Tie a string to the screw hook and loop the other end through the bottle cap so both ends are secure. You want the string length to be short enough that the ball is not hitting the ground when the child is playing with the toy.

For the Play-Together Game
Remove the stringed Ping-Pong ball from the plastic bottle, make a second cup catcher and use an untethered Ping-Pong ball to fling back and forth.

Modifications for Younger Kids
Have younger kids play on the floor and try to capture the rolling Ping-Pong ball under the cup.

Modifications for Older Kids
This is a great activity for older kids that really challenges them. Have them come up with rules for both games so they can keep score.

Topsy Turvy Game

My grandpa had a desktop toy that I loved to play with when I visited. It was a set of metal rods that were on a slight decline with a metal ball. By placing the ball at the bottom of the hill and carefully moving the rods in and out, I could cautiously propel the ball upward.

This two-person game is inspired by that desktop game featuring gravity. Using two pool noodles and a discount store ball, the object is to move the rods to propel the ball into a bucket.

Materials
+ 2 POOL NOODLES
+ 2 BUCKETS
+ LIGHTWEIGHT BALL

TIP
Working together on ball movement strategies can help kids develop the skills to manage a task without fighting.

The two players face each other and hold the ends of the pool noodles in each hand. A bucket is placed at the feet of each participant. The ball is positioned on top of the pool noodles.

Players work together to move the ball to one end and drop the ball into the bucket and then back again to the other bucket. This teamwork game is more about the process than the score.

Modifications for Younger Kids
Pair younger kids with an older partner to assist their movements and coordinate ball movement.

Modifications for Older Kids
Older kids can assign one partner to be stationary and not change the position of their end of the pool noodles, creating a challenge for the other player to move the ball toward the stationary partner's bucket. Score can be kept from the results.

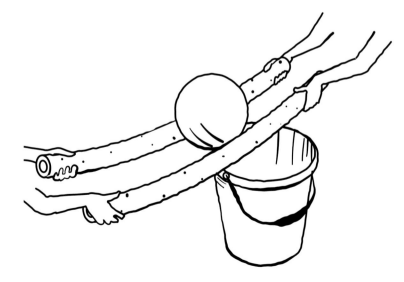

Human Jousting

This was the way my brother and I solved conflict as older kids. If one was really frustrated with the other, he or she would call for a joust to settle it. I think it works for two reasons: there are times when you really want to hit your brother. There are times when a little humor will put in perspective the issue at hand.

This activity is just plain silly fun with or without conflict. It also will have any spectators in stitches as they watch two people armed with hand face shields and waving, uncoordinated arm spears joust until it is broken by laughter.

The participants stretch their right arm out in front of them, with their right hand about eye level. The left arm wraps underneath the outstretched right arm and the left hand comes up to cover the face entirely.

The right arm is now the spear. The left hand is the face shield.

Participants face each other and take three steps back. Maintaining spear and shield form, they move toward each other to fight until laughter.

Modifications for Younger Kids

Younger kids may need help wrapping themselves up into the proper form and should be paired with an opponent who fights gently.

Modifications for Older Kids

Set up a tournament where the winner of each bout is the person who didn't smile the longest. A silly bracket of events can be a fun party activity.

Red Light Run

Red Light, Green Light is the first organized game that I remember playing as a child. The excitement of sneaking forward to the goal when the caller's back was turned felt like getting away with something dangerous.

One step. Two steps. I will try three . . . *oh no!*

Each game was unconsciously a study in predictions and reading people.

We love this traditional game and have a modern twist that starts with a craft to create a contemporary signal light.

Materials
(to make one red light)

+ Tissue box
+ 2 or 3 sheets of white construction paper
+ Tape or glue
+ Lid for tracing
+ 1 sheet each red, yellow and green construction paper
+ Scissors
+ Dark marker

Cover the tissue box with the white paper and tape or glue in place. Using a small lid, trace circles onto the red, yellow and green paper. Cut out four circles in each of the colors. To make it obvious which "light" was lit, we drew dark lines over half of the "lights."

Secure the circles to the box as the lights. We made sure three of the sides only had one light "visible" or without lines on it. On the fourth side we added a "one-way" arrow to tell the kids to turn around.

Have one child roll the "light." The rest of the kids should be at a line across the room/field. Whatever the light says the kids get to do. For example, if it is "green" they run very fast. If it is yellow they walk slowly. Red they freeze. The race changes as fast as the roller can turn the light. The coveted position in our family was being the light post.

Modifications for Younger Kids

Younger kids don't have to abide by the freeze rule between rolls. They can run free until the next light is chosen.

Younger participants can also be given a head start of time or number of rolls before the older kids join the game.

This game is a great way for young kids to practice listening to simple instructions. It's a great game to help prepare your kids for walking in parking lots or other potentially dangerous areas by using the same instructions as the game commands: "red light—stop" or "yellow—be careful and walk slowly" or "green—you are good to go play."

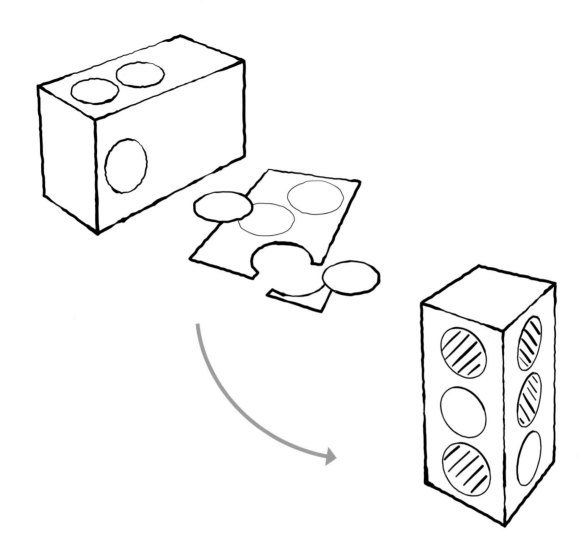

Modifications for Older Kids

For older participants, add more structure to the game. Try creating roads or paths that they need to drive on. Add some street rules, like they can only pass on the right, or that they have to come to a complete stop before they turn, and so forth.

Shoe Box Pinball

The flashing lights, the music and that elusive ring, ring, ring when the goal is hit makes even watching pinball fun. But deep down in every pinball player is the desire to conquer the coordination it requires and the timing that it demands.

This DIY pinball game starts as a shoe box craft and transforms into a game of coordination. When the game is over, it can be easily stored back in its shoe box shell.

Materials
(to make one game)

+ Scissors
+ 2 foam sheets with sticker backs, or plain foam
+ Cardboard or cardstock—may be needed to stiffen the foam sheets
+ Glue (if the foam lacks a sticky back)
+ 6 unsharpened pencils
+ 1 sharpened pencil
+ Shoe box lid
+ Tape
+ Marble or small bouncy ball

Cut a foam strip approximately 1 inch (2.5 cm) wide and 5 inches (12.5 cm) long. If the foam doesn't keep its shape well, then cut a cardboard strip that is 1 inch (2.5 cm) wide and 2 inches (5 cm) long. Peel the backing off the foam (or cover the foam with a light layer of glue) and place an unsharpened pencil halfway down the length of the foam strip just under the eraser. Fold the foam together over the pencil, sandwiching the cardboard strip.

Using the sharpened pencil, push through the bottom of the shoe box, creating holes to put the paddles in that can be controlled from below. Insert the unsharpened pencil "paddles" into the holes.

At each end make a hole for a goal and outline with tape.

Each player uses the paddles to advance the ball toward the goal at the opposite end of the shoe box.

The player that makes five goals first, wins.

Modifications for Younger Kids
This is a fun solo game when made with only one goal. Kids can figure out which pencils they need to move to hit the ball above.

This is a simple way for kids to see cause and reaction. A movement below the box can change the course of the ball in the box. Use differently color pencils to help identify which pencil is causing which action.

Modifications for Older Kids
Designing the box ahead of time to give each player a certain number of pencils to control like a foosball game can make it more competitive and fair. Using a larger box and setting it up on the backs of two chairs can stabilize the game for play.

Team Banded Together

In high school I attended a leadership camp for three glorious days of team-building exercises. As a team we scaled walls, went through obstacles and caught one another as we fell backward off a platform. I was in team-loving heaven.

The family is the ultimate team. A group of people born to work together! This series of activities using a stretchy T-shirt band can help build team family!

Materials

+ Stretchy material like old T-shirts or sportlike material
+ Sewing machine (optional)

TIP

Do you have two kids who are constantly at war? Use an activity like this to team them up against a parent and watch how a common goal can overcome differences.

Using strips from old T-shirts or purchased material with a good stretch, create a band that is 12 to 18 inches (30.5 to 45.5 cm) wide and 12 feet (3.7 m) long. Sew the ends of the 12-foot (3.7 m) -long strip together to create a complete circle. Using knots to bind the ends together will work as well. It needs to be strong . . . *it is about to get tested!*

Gather the participants together on a soft playing surface. Three or four players works well, and backyard lawn is the perfect surface.

One person is designated as the coach and will give the directions. The other players get inside the band, placing the band at waist level.

The kids' first impulse is to run in opposite directions inside the band. This in itself will take a minute to sort out.

Stretchy Band Games

- **Taxi Game:** Have the driver be the smallest child in a multi-age situation. The driver is to go in one direction as fast as possible while the other kids move to the "back" of the band and try to slow down the driver—without making the driver fall.

- **Shape Creation:** Shout out a shape for the kids to make and watch as the kids try to shift to fashion that shape with the band. Depending on the number in the band, this can take some balance and thought.

- **Obstacle Course:** Set up a few obstacles that the team must successfully negotiate to cross the "finish line"—together.

- **Big Boss:** Have a coach call out directions such as "Turn right," "Rotate to the left," "Switch leaders," "Walk backward," and so on. The participants follow the commands while maintaining the band around their waists.

- **Impossi-pull:** Everyone in the loop pulls away from the center, but only at the resistance of the smallest member. It takes adjusting to keep the pressure at a strength that accommodates all.

Modifications for Younger Kids

The stretchier the fabric, the more unexpected force can happen from the band. Make sure that if there is a large gap in participant size, an older child or parent is working from the inside to make sure the smaller participant is not being run over. One easy way to do that is to place that younger child in charge of leading the group or giving instructions.

Modifications for Older Kids

Older kids can be the "coach" or buddy of smaller participants in multi-age/size scenarios. When older kids play together, the instructions and obstacles can be more complicated, emphasizing the need to communicate as a team to finish the task.

Want to make this game more complicated for older kids? Mix this activity with the Red Light Run (page 136).

Tin Can Target

My kids are simply noisy. It doesn't seem to matter how many times I hush them; at some point in the day they will be sent outside to expend all that sound energy. The other thing that goes along with all that noise is the innate need to throw things. "No throwing inside the house" is a reminder that is given daily. This game incorporates both childish tendencies, along with items from our recycle bin to create a fun musical game.

We use recycled tin cans as targets for throwing spoons, rewarding those who hit the cans with a delightful ring.

Materials

+ EMPTY, CLEAN TIN CANS, IN A VARIETY OF SHAPES AND SIZES
+ SANDPAPER OR WIDE, STURDY TAPE
+ NAIL
+ HAMMER
+ ROPE
+ BOLT
+ LOTS OF ICE CREAM SPOONS
+ PAINT AND EMBELLISHMENTS (OPTIONAL)

Make sure the inside of the can is free of sharp edges by smoothing with sandpaper or covering them with sturdy tape. Use a nail and hammer to make a hole in the closed end of the can. Thread one end of the rope through the hole and tie the bolt on the end inside the can. Use an ice cream spoon to fix the bolt in a ringer position by adding it several inches above the bolt to stop rope slippage through the hole. Your child has now created a can "bell." Repeat the process until you have a collection of different size "bells" for your children to hit.

We made our cans easier to spot and more fun to bang with decorations. With the help of paint, stickers and bands of tape we decorated our cans.

Modifications for Younger Kids

For younger kids, enjoy watching them run around banging on the tin can bells. You can also make it easier for them by placing the bells close together. You can encourage your children to create a pattern or a rhythm with their banging, or ask them to work with a partner to create a "song" together.

Modifications for Older Kids

Find a place to hang the bells. We used the trees in our backyard, but a ladder or even a fence can work well if there are no trees or hanging hooks available. Each player is given an equal stack of spoons. They stand on a designated spot away from the target and throw the spoon, trying to hit the can. A ring of the bell counts as a point, which is signified by moving one of their remaining spoons into a "point pile." The player who runs out of spoons first, wins.

The Great Toy Toss

Did all the toy bins at your house explode?

Never fear, The Great Toy Toss is coming to the rescue. This game will get kids working together toward a clean-up cause with nary a complaint. Kids can be paired together or work in teams to launch stuffed animals toward a laundry basket goal.

Materials

+ 2 PILLOWCASES
+ COLLECTION OF STUFFED ANIMALS
+ LAUNDRY BASKET OR TOY BIN

TIP

When you make cleanup into a game it helps reenergize kiddos and brings a smile to what otherwise might be a disappointing time of the day. We also sing "cleanup" songs to cue our preschoolers that it is "time to work."

Two kids each hold the end of a pillowcase. It is positioned like a stretcher with a toy placed in the middle.

Kids work together to bounce a toy into the air with the aim of landing it in the desired laundry basket goal.

A Silly Work-Together Game with 2 Kids

The two kids work together to launch the stuffed animals into the goal. You "win" when your toys make it into the bin! Work toward 100 percent accuracy for a group of animal projectiles.

The Great Toy Toss with 4+ Kids

Have two or more teams. Have team A call for a toy from team B. Team A tosses the toy without touching it, with the help of the pillowcase. Team B tries to catch the toy on their pillowcase, then drops it into the toy bin.

To increase the difficulty, set two laundry baskets on opposite sides of the room, with each team trying to get animals in their respective goals. Animals from the opposite team need to be bounced into the goal while animals from their pile need to be bounced to the opposite team's pillowcase trampoline.

Modifications for Younger Kids

Use the pillowcase to create a toy trampoline. No need for a goal; this is just plain fun!

For the youngest participants, hide the toy underneath the pillowcase. Watch your child play peek-a-boo with the toy.

Modifications for Older Kids

Teams can create an elaborate bounce obstacle course or pattern that the toy needs to go through to get to the goal. For instance, they may require the first trampoline to bounce the toy three times and then launch to the other player or team that has to take the toy in three rotations before launching back. Let kids get creative with instructions, which will become surprisingly complicated!

Watch It Fall

There is a part inside each of us that wants to get away with something. To make a mess. To cause a disaster. To just "see what would happen if . . ." We would love to cause a chain reaction, defy nature or stop the inevitable. It is an intense willing against the unavoidable.

This is a simple game created from kitchen utensils and recyclables that will have family members holding their breath as they test their ability to stop what is certain to happen.

Materials

+ Pom-poms or packing peanuts
+ Large spaghetti strainer
+ Package of pipe cleaners or wooden skewers
+ Something to balance the strainer on (e.g., books or blocks)

Place a layer of pom-poms or packing peanuts in the bottom of the strainer to approximately 4 inches (10 cm) deep. Push pipe cleaners through one side of the strainer and out the other. Continuing to add pipe cleaners at random angles until the strainer can be turned over without the pom-poms falling out. Turn the strainer upside down and place on several books or blocks so that the underside of the strainer can be seen.

Each player takes a turn pulling out the pipe cleaner of his/her choice. If the removal causes pom-poms to fall, then those fallen pom-poms are placed in front of that player. At the end of the game, the person who has the smallest pile of fallen pom-poms wins.

Modifications for Younger Kids
Don't worry about trying to stop the pom-poms from falling; let the kids watch as their actions cause reactions. Tots will enjoy playing with them even without the "rules" of the game. If your tot still puts small items in his mouth, play "threading" and watch your child gain fine motor skills as he threads pipe cleaners in the colander.

Modifications for Older Kids
Let older kids set up the game with the goal of finding a strategy for pulling the most pipe cleaners out without any pom-poms falling.

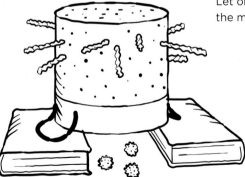

Water Bomb Games

Sponges, with just a couple of adaptations, make a great toy to use in a variety of water games. We have enjoyed our sponge water "bombs" in the bathtub, tried to avoid getting wet in a game of Sponge Dodgeball and played Duck, Duck, Goose . . . only "Goose" was "You're wet! Bet you can't catch me!"

This activity creates a sponge bomb and adds a few suggestions for games to play.

Materials
(makes two water bombs)

+ Scissors
+ 5 differently colored sponges
+ Sturdy string

Cut the sponges lengthwise. You can get three or four strips from most sponges. Stack half of the sponge strips together, mixing the colored strips for variety. Very tightly, tie the string around the center of the stacked sponges. As you cinch the string and knot it, the sponge strips should bunch out—like a giant pom-pom.

Grab a bucket of water, some kids and have fun!

Sponge Dodgeball
Have your children try to get you or their friends "out" by hitting them with the wet sponge balls.

Duck, Duck, Goose
Have your children sit in a circle as they play this classic game. As the child walks around the circumference of the circle, saying, "Duck, Duck," have her lightly touch the kids as she walks . . . but when it comes to "Goose," have the child who is "It" squeeze the water sponge onto the "Goose." "Jail" can be a kiddie pool in the center filled with water.

Paint Pollock Style
Fill a couple of buckets with a variety of colors of sidewalk paint (page 77). Put the sponge balls into the buckets. When the kids want to paint with that color, have them throw the paint-soaked ball at the sidewalk, or sling paint along the way. Hose off your children and the walkway when you are finished.

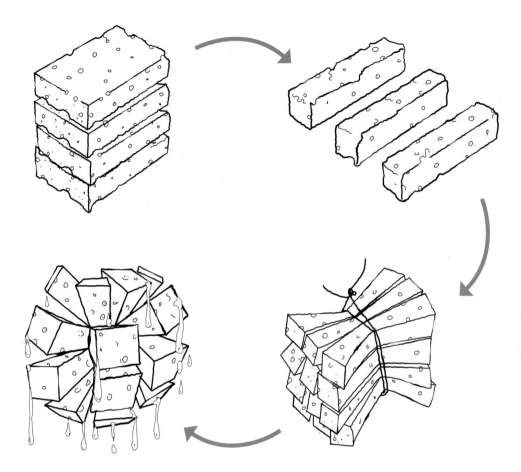

Modifications for Younger Kids

Different-size sponge strips will create different textures of Sponge Bombs—play around with the design. You can even use dish rags or cut-up pieces of felt or fleece and add these to your balls. These make great sensory toys when dry to let tots explore what each feels like.

Throw a couple of these into the tub for a fun bathtime game. When dry, these are great quiet toys to have in the diaper bag for a young tot.

Modifications for Older Kids

Leave a bucket of these at the door and welcome your children home to a game of Sponge Ball "War." They will love you for it!

(four)

SIMPLE SCIENCE

Science is play at its most curious. It looks at something ordinary and explores the whys and hows behind it. Children's natural examination of the world can be emboldened when their questions are a catalyst for playing with science.

Holly's Pick: I am always amazed by the magic of vinegar plus baking soda, which is why my favorite science activities are Sandbox Volcano (page 175), Fizzy Color Drop (page 165) and Fizzy Sidewalk Paint (page 162).

Rachel's Pick: Of all the science experiments we have done over the years, Naked Eggs (page 173) stick out in my kids' memories. They got to touch, see, feel and experience a cell—physically. I love how science encourages curiosity and respect for the world around them!

Archaeology Dig with Supersoft Dough

Searching for treasures is a basic human desire. The delight of discovery is real whether it be prehistoric bones on an archeological dig or a plastic toy buried in play dough. This homemade dough is one of my favorites. It is sweet smelling and soft to the touch, which makes it the perfect medium for an archeological toy dig.

Materials
(to make one dig site)

+ Medium-size bowl
+ About ½ cup (120 ml) leftover hair conditioner (see Tip)
+ About 1 cup (128 g) cornstarch
+ Glitter and food dye (optional)
+ Baking dish
+ Little toys (e.g., dinosaurs)
+ Archeology tools (e.g., coffee stirrers, toothpicks and/or spoons)

TIP
Do you have leftover sunscreen from last summer? You can replace the hair conditioner in this recipe with any lotion.

In a medium-size bowl, mix the conditioner and cornstarch together until it is the consistency of play dough. The amounts vary depending on the type of conditioner. Typically, you need about ½ cup (120 ml) of conditioner to 1 cup (128 g) of cornstarch. If it is too sticky, add more cornstarch; if it is crumbly or hard, add more conditioner.

Half the fun is mixing the ingredients. Add glitter for an extra sparkle. Food dye to color the dough is optional. Store in an airtight bag. Add small amounts of conditioner or oil to the dough after it has been stored to rehydrate the dough before playing with it.

In preparation for the dig, layer the bottom of a baking dish with your dinos. Press the soft dough over the tops of your toys. Try to extricate the toys, leaving as little remaining dough on the items, using "tools" found in your kitchen.

Modifications for Younger Kids
Add a tablespoon (15 ml) of oil to the dough. It will help the objects be removed more easily.

Modifications for Older Kids
Have them try multiple batches, and see whether it is easier or harder to perform an archeology dig in a moist dough or a crumbly one. Experience the problems that archeologists face due to soil conditions.

Book Bridge Building

Anyone who has built with wooden blocks has been intrigued by the mystery of the bridge architecture. *How does it span that distance without falling in the middle?* It is a question that can spur hours of building, in hopes of discovering the answer.

This is a favorite activity because we always have what we need on hand. We use the books we already own and two dining room chairs as the building materials for our architectural bridge design. Kids will play with the concept of span and innately problem solve complex mathematical questions while placing books through trial and error. They can build various types of bridges (beam, truss, cantilever) and see which works best.

Materials

+ 25 OR MORE HARDCOVER BOOKS
+ 2 CHAIRS

Examine a bridge next time you are out driving with your child. Discuss how the base starts before the actual bridge does. When home, recreate a bridge by beginning with a base with the books and then moving each subsequent book closer and closer to the center while not dropping any books.

Modifications for Younger Kids

Younger kids can build a shorter bridge on the floor and experiment with how to create a span that is slightly wider than a book length.

Put your treasured books on a high shelf during this activity and start with the kids' books. Younger kids will drop and dent books during play—so prepare by giving them the books that won't be harmed or worried about.

Modifications for Older Kids

Add variety, use chairs of different sizes and watch your child problem solve and adapt the bridge to span different gaps.

Test the strength of your bridge by building a tower over the top of your bridge. The extra books are weight. How does it hold up?

If you have a large personal library, then give the kids a challenge to get across the kitchen floor with the use of only three chairs and a stack of books. Give them a problem to solve that seems just a little bit impossible.

CD Spinning Top

There is a reason why spinning top toys have been popular as long as there have been children. They are easy to make with just about any type of material, and they have a coolness factor that is ageless.

This modern version spins around a marble axis with a little pickup from gyroscopic action. It stays upright as long as the inertia can keep up the speed needed to avoid toppling. This activity is simple to assemble and can teach your kids about color theory and the way our brains automatically mix colors—fascinating.

Materials

+ SMALL MARBLE
+ MODELING CLAY—ROUGHLY THE AMOUNT OF TWO STICKS OF GUM
+ OLD CD
+ PERMANENT MARKERS (OPTIONAL)
+ STICKERS (OPTIONAL)

TIP

Play with the CDs as reflectors. Have kids shine a flashlight on the CD as it spins. Watch the light dance on the ceiling. Give the kids a point on a wall to try to illuminate and see what it takes to make that happen. Talk to your kids about angles and try to predict where the light will bounce if you change the position of the flashlight.

Stick the marble into a quarter-size (roughly 2.5 cm-diameter) piece of clay and then stuff that into the CD hole. The marble should be mostly exposed. You do not want to cover the whole marble with clay. Place your creation on a smooth surface; balance the CD on the marble and spin! Watch it swirl!

Color Mash

Using markers, color one half of the CD with one primary color and the other half with a different primary color. Watch the colors combine into a secondary color when spinning as your brain mixes the colors together.

Spin Marathon

See who can keep the top spinning for the longest time. Explain to your child how centrifugal force helps your spinning CD resist the laws of gravity; as long as the force of the turn is greater than the force of gravity, the CD will not "topple."

Modifications for Younger Kids

Younger kids can practice the movement required to set the top in motion. If they are too young to successfully get the top spinning, then having them try to stop a spinning top can be lots of fun.

Modifications for Older Kids

Have older kids make several tops and try to keep at least one of them in motion for a set amount of time. It will test their ability to predict which top is slowing down and try to judge which top requires immediate attention.

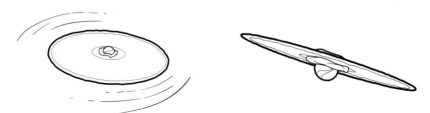

Compost Soup

One of my favorite childhood stories is *Stone Soup*. It shows how ingredients that aren't much on their own can be combined into something that blesses an entire community. That story is in the back of my head when we create compost soup. Any one of the composting ingredients on its own is considered trash, but when they are combined they make a wonderful "soup" for garden worms.

This activity is a way for kids to really get involved in the composting process in mixing and creating a final product that will be a blessing to any garden. Four things are needed for composting organisms to be able to work their magic: carbon (brown and dry matter), nitrogen (wet green and colorful matter), oxygen (mixing it so the air can get in) and water (grab a watering can).

Materials

+ Giant bowl or big tub
+ A collection of spoons and scoops
+ Dirt
+ Grass clippings
+ Sawdust
+ Eggshells
+ Vegetable scraps
+ Dryer lint
+ Coffee grounds
+ Stale bread crumbs
+ Other compostable items

Head outside and grab a giant bowl or big tub and a variety of spoons and scoops, along with your bucket of scraps.

Think outside the box with biodegradable items to include in your compost bin. We have included shredded 100 percent cotton clothes, toilet paper tubes, stale candy and *tons* of other items. It is great to feed the plants and worms while lessening our trash.

Mash, mix and stir all the compost ingredients into a gloriously messy compost soup.

We like to use pretend dishes for a pretend worm tea party. When the kids are done mixing their soup, they can pour cupfuls of the compost around the plants in your garden, giving them a nutritious snack.

Modifications for Younger Kids
Younger kids can help remind the family of compostable materials to save in the kitchen. They are really good at a mission!

Modifications for Older Kids
Older kids can create their own unique composting mix to put on their part of the garden to see whether they can improve plant growth.

Cork Boats & a Tinfoil River

With this activity, kids will innately learn about water displacement and how to weight and shape a boat in different ways for different results. They can test their hypothesis about which ship will sail the best and which will flip and sink. Because these cork boats are so simple, you can make a fleet!

Materials

+ KNIFE
+ CORKS—EACH CORK MAKES 2 BOATS
+ 1 OR 2 TOOTHPICKS PER BOAT
+ STURDY TAPE
+ RUBBER BANDS
+ TINFOIL
+ DRINKING STRAWS (OPTIONAL)

To make a simple sailboat: Cut the cork in half lengthwise. Stick a toothpick into the center of the cork and use the tape to fashion a sail.

To make a weight-bearing raft: Use tape or rubber bands to secure a line of corks to one another. Add toothpicks and tape for sails. You will want to try a number of variations. See how many corks you can unite to create the most stable ship, or which arrangement will sail the fastest.

Optional: To make a river: Cut a long length of tinfoil for your kids to play with. Roll the edges so the foil will hold water. Place the river outside and add some water. This doesn't have to be running water; you can create more of a lakelike river. Place the cork boats in the water.

Figure out a way to sail the boats "down" the river. It could be by adding cups of water to one end of the river or having the kids use a straw to sail the ships toward a goal.

Get out a stopwatch and see how long it will take for your boats to make it to the finish line.

Modifications for Younger Kids
Give them a cup of water to pour and keep each boat floating downriver. Let them use their hands as the boat's motor.

This activity works well as a solo (or small people pair) activity in the bathtub.

Modifications for Older Kids
Older kids can work on not only an offensive race with a straw, but a defensive race as well. Allow them to attempt to blow their competition out of the water. Literally.

DIY Bouncy Ball

The ingredients needed to create these bouncy balls are not bouncy in and of themselves. As you collect the ingredients for your balls, look at the textures—glue is sticky and cornstarch is powdery. Neither one can bounce on its own. The molecules of the ingredients are small and generally incomplete. But when you add a catalyst to the glue, starch and water, it transforms the characteristic properties of these ingredients—creating a rubbery-textured polymer. To make this ball, your kids just linked and mixed molecules together.

A quick word of caution: this recipe includes borax, which is not edible. Please don't let children chew on the finished product or taste it during any steps along the way.

Materials
(to make two bouncy balls)

+ 4 TABLESPOONS (60 ML) WARM WATER
+ 1 TEASPOON BORAX (FIND IT IN THE LAUNDRY DETERGENT SECTION OF YOUR LOCAL STORE)
+ 2 DISPOSABLE CUPS
+ DISPOSABLE SPOON, FOR STIRRING
+ 2 TABLESPOONS (30 ML) GLUE
+ 2 TABLESPOONS (16 G) CORNSTARCH
+ FOOD COLORING (OPTIONAL)
+ MEASURING SPOONS

TIP
The ingredients and instructions to make a homemade bouncy ball make a great gift when packaged together in a small plastic bucket.

First pour the water and borax into the first cup and stir the mixture until it is dissolved.

Next, pour the glue, cornstarch, food coloring and ½ teaspoon (2.5 ml) of the mixture from the first cup into the second cup. After the cornstarch and glue are mixed together pour contents of cup #2 into cup #1. Our ball recipe seems to work best if you mix the glue, cornstarch and food coloring first, and *then* pour it into the borax mixture.

Let the ingredients in the second cup interact on their own for about 15 seconds, then stir. We found that a folding method was the most effective way to stir the ingredients. Once the mixture becomes difficult to stir, scoop it out of the cup and roll it into a ball. There will be a watery borax mixture left in the container. You will want to dispose of that liquid and throw away the container.

We stored it in a resealable plastic bag for several days and it stayed fresh until it simply picked up too much dirt and we had to throw it out!

Modifications for Younger Kids
Younger children can have fun bouncing the balls—see which one of them can bounce their ball the highest.

Modifications for Older Kids
Older kids can test different sizes to make modifications to elicit more bounce action. Encourage your kids to tweak the ingredients—how does the ball change if you add more or less of just one ingredient? They can also test out different shapes and how that affects how the ball bounces. We found that this is a forgiving recipe—almost all of our versions bounced to some degree.

Fizzing Sidewalk Paint

This activity trumps ordinary sidewalk chalk with a little science magic by creating a chalk-based paint and then spritzing on a little fizz. It all starts with pH. When solutions that are pH base mix with an acid, action happens!

Materials

+ Large mixing bowl
+ 1 (1-pound [454 g]) box baking soda
+ 1/2 cup (63 g) cornstarch
+ Warm water
+ Several containers to hold the paint
+ Food coloring
+ Paintbrush(es)
+ Spray bottle filled with vinegar—1 per child
+ Buckets for cleanup

TIP

Do you have a prewriting preschooler? Use a turkey baster to squirt vinegar at the paint. The grasping and squeezing helps strengthen finger muscles they will use when they are writing.

In a large mixing bowl, mix the baking soda and the cornstarch together. Add the warm (almost hot) water, stirring until it is the consistency of pancake batter. Split the recipe into several containers, adding the food coloring color of your choice to each.

Use the homemade paint to create a scene or flick it with a paintbrush into a modern masterpiece. It is best to work fast because the paint dries quickly (but can always be diluted with the addition of more warm water).

Once the painting is in place, it is time for something a little extra. Spray the artwork with the vinegar-filled bottle and watch what happens.

Your artwork will sizzle and pop!

About Cleanup

A bucketful of water splashed across the art can make it disappear. Because that is fun, too, you might not want to wait for rain.

Modifications for Younger Kids

If a paintbrush is hard to negotiate in the paint, give your children a spoon and let them drip or drop spoonfuls of paint onto the pavement. For the little ones, be sure to fully supervise when they spray vinegar. It can sting little eyes.

Modifications for Older Kids

This activity is an easy way to work in a lesson on reactions between acids and base chemicals and talk about why this works. Maybe you can have your budding scientists adapt the recipe to see whether they can get bigger bubbles and more fizz in their next batch of paint.

Fizzy Color Drop

Baking soda and vinegar go together like peas and carrots . . . well, in my house they are more popular than peas and carrots, but that is a whole other issue.

The amazing play experience that happens when you use baking soda as a canvas for colorful vinegar drops equals a good hour of intense and exploratory fun. When baking soda (base) and vinegar (acid) combine, they become carbonic acid. The carbonic acid is so unstable that it quickly falls apart, resulting in bubbles of carbon dioxide. These are the same type of bubbles that cause quick breads to rise.

This is a really good rainy-day activity. If the sun is shining, move outside to enjoy it.

Materials

+ BAKING SHEET OR FLAT PLASTIC CONTAINER
+ 1 (1-POUND [454 G]) BOX BAKING SODA
+ PLASTIC CUPS
+ 1 TO 2 CUPS (235 TO 475 ML) VINEGAR
+ FOOD COLORING
+ MEDICINE DROPPERS, PLASTIC SYRINGES OR TURKEY BASTER

Cover the bottom of a baking sheet or flat plastic container with a ½-inch (2.5 cm) -deep layer of baking soda.

In plastic cups, fill each partially with vinegar and a different food coloring color.

Using a medicine dropper or plastic syringe, fill it with the colored vinegar mixture and drop it onto the baking soda canvas. Watch as the colorful fizzing reaction happens. Play with the colors to make new colors as they bubble.

Modifications for Younger Kids

If the medicine dropper or plastic syringe is a challenge to control, consider using an ear bulb, which is more easily grasped by little hands.

Alternatively, put the drops of food coloring onto the baking sheet, then cover lightly with the baking soda. Let your child use a spoon to drop teaspoonfuls (5 ml) of vinegar onto the white canvas and see a surprise burst of color emerge.

Modifications for Older Kids

Creating a temporary masterpiece, such as a rainbow or another scene, by dropping the colors can be a playful challenge. Take a picture of the final product.

Slimy Copy Machine with Goop Recipe

The Sunday paper was the absolute best way to test the duplicating powers of Silly Putty. If you did it just right, you could create a color copy of a favorite comic. The ink used in newspapers has changed over time, resulting in less than perfect copies, but you can revive the experience in your own home with pencil drawings.

We are channeling those early Sunday experiences with this fun recipe to make homemade putty and then use it to copy images, text or textures. All sorts of fun!

Materials

+ SMALL BOWL
+ ½ TEASPOON (5 G) BORAX
+ ¼ CUP (60 ML) WARM WATER
+ ¼ CUP (32 G) CORNSTARCH
+ 2 TO 3 OUNCES (60 TO 90 ML) WHITE GLUE (ROUGHLY ½ OF A 4-OUNCE [120 ML] CONTAINER)
+ FOOD COLORING (LIQUID KIND)
+ DURABLE, RESEALABLE PLASTIC FREEZER BAG
+ SPOON, FOR MIXING
+ A VARIETY OF PRINTED PAPERS AND WRITING MEDIUMS

In a small bowl, dissolve the borax in the water; set aside.

Combine the borax mixture with the remaining ingredients in a durable resealable plastic freezer bag.

The mix will seem clumpy and stringy, but mix for several minutes, until all the ingredients are combined.

Let it sit for 30 minutes or longer. Give the cornstarch time to absorb the moisture before kneading the bag again. We found it takes about 20 to 30 minutes of kneading to gain a putty consistency.

Roll your homemade putty out until it is flat. Find different pages with writing on them. Press the pages into the goop and see the mirrored image retained by the goop.

Try a variety of different texts, papers and writing mediums. Which sticks better? Pencil? Pen? Marker? Experiment by writing on the goop and transferring it back to the paper.

Modifications for Younger Kids

Leave the borax out of the recipe. The goop will have a different consistency, but this adaptation will make the recipe nontoxic if ingested. Borax is laundry detergent booster and is not edible.

Modifications for Older Kids

Change the amount of cornstarch that you add . . . using all of the ingredients, you can create slime (use more glue and water, less cornstarch) and bouncy balls (page 161).

TIP

Want a fun way to store your goop? Fill balloons with your slimy mixture. It will keep longer in the balloon and be a fun, mess-less way to squish the goop until you are ready to play with it again.

Hydrofoils

The simple concepts behind how things float are fun to explore. They turn a sink or bathtub into a science laboratory. It all starts with boat design. Then testing of that design. Then making informed alterations and starting all over again.

Water holds together in such a way that it creates a pressure that pushes things up. Gravity wants to pull the boat down. The result is a cosmic fight we call buoyancy. Overcome gravity or harness the power of density to avoid sinking.

This activity uses water (hydro) and tinfoil (foil) to test your little boat designers' skills.

Materials
+ TINFOIL
+ JAR OF COINS
+ SINK, BUCKET OR BATHTUB

Give each participant a similarly sized piece of tinfoil and have them fashion it into a structure that will float. Each prototype can be tested in the water and modifications made by folding and smushing (totally a scientific word) the moldable foil. Once the design is satisfactory, then it is time for testing.

Next, the participants start adding coins to their design to see how many they can add before the design fails and sinks. If everyone is using pennies, then you can easily keep track of which design held up the best by counting the money that it holds.

Modifications for Younger Kids
This is the perfect bathtub experiment. Younger kids can create a fleet of boats with several pieces of tinfoil and then attempt to let their other bath toys float on their boats.

Modifications for Older Kids
Have older kids hypothesize as to which design will hold up the best and then compete in the testing. Let them research buoyancy and then test their findings.

Introduce waves to the test by carefully adding water (rain—mimicking a storm) to show how a little water over a short boat side can have disastrous effects.

Milk Explosions

This activity uses milk and food coloring to create art. The milk fat holds the color until dish soap breaks the tension of the fat, releasing the dye throughout the milk in a burst of color. Because of this unique property, milk can be used to create fascinating artworks.

Materials

+ WHOLE MILK (CREAM IS EVEN BETTER!)
+ DISH
+ MULTIPLE COLORS OF FOOD COLORING
+ COTTON SWAB OR TOOTHPICK
+ LIQUID DISH SOAP
+ SEVERAL PIECES OF CARDSTOCK

Pour the milk into a dish. You don't want a whole lot, just enough to cover the bottom of your dish. Add drops of food dye, then dip a cotton swab into the soap and lightly touch the surface of the milk. Watch the milk explode in color. As the colors are swirling, dip a piece of cardstock into the milk. You should have a very lightly patterned swirl on your paper. Your child captured the milk explosion!

For a more evident keepsake of this experiment, dip a second piece of cardstock into the milk; make sure the page is good and wet. It's okay for it to have puddles even. This is a messy project. Drop a drip of food coloring onto the milky page. The dye should stay pretty stationary where you put it. Dab the center of the "drip" with soap and watch the ink run away from your swab. Repeat across the sheet with a variety of colors.

We were pleased with the shiny card that was the result of our morning with science.

Modifications for Younger Kids

Have an adult do the food dye drips. You only want one or two, as those bottles are hard to control. Have them work with one color at a time.

Modifications for Older Kids

Do a science experiment: use 2% milk, whole milk and cream. Which one isolates the dye the most? Which one spreads the dye most easily? Why?

Have your older children personalize the finished work with embellishments—transform the paper into postcards to mail to a friend.

This technique can be used to create a colorful canvas for more art. Let the first layer dry and then further illustrate the design with markers or more paint.

Naked Egg Experiment

This activity puts a cell in the hands of kids. They can see, touch, even pop the membrane with their fingers, and explore how the cell's permeable membrane diffuses molecules (i.e., stays hydrated) in a way they understand.

The acetic acid in the vinegar breaks up the calcium carbonate crystals in the eggshell. At the end of this experiment, you will have a naked egg! (We advise that you start with at least three or four eggs because your child will break one or more; eggs without their shells are very fragile.)

Materials
(to make one naked egg [see headnote])

+ 3 OR 4 EGGS
+ LARGE GLASS BOWL
+ 1 CUP (235 ML) VINEGAR

TIPS

In addition to being a great science experiment, Naked Eggs can be a fun prank for the little cook in your life. Put a collection of naked eggs into the egg carton. They will be shocked to pull out a giant, slimy egg where they were expecting a normal one. p.s. While the naked eggs are edible and were even considered to be a delicacy in ancient eras, from experience we warn you, they taste foul. We would not advise using them in a recipe.

This experiment takes several days to complete. To begin, place your eggs in a large glass bowl. You will want to leave about an inch (2.5 cm) of space between each egg because they are going to swell as their shell dissolves. Cover the eggs with roughly an inch (2.5 cm) of vinegar. The eggs will float. Watch. Almost immediately you will see the eggs begin to spin and bubbles rise to the surface. The bubbles are the release of gas. The shells are a base and the vinegar is an acid—combined base and acid elements create gas (or bubbles). If you put a piece of plastic wrap over your bowl, you will see it balloon up as it fills with gas. You will want to keep your eggs in the vinegar for three days, to fully dissolve the shell. As the shell disintegrates in the vinegar you can see the membrane and witness the egg expand. The egg is expanding as the vinegar (water) is diffused by osmosis into the egg, causing it to swell.

Modifications for Younger Kids
Let them enjoy gently holding the naked egg. Don't be surprised if the egg bursts. They are fragile in their shell-free state.

Modifications for Older Kids
Take one of the naked eggs and put it into a sugar solution (corn syrup, flat soda, even juice). Watch what happens to the egg after it sits in the sugar all day. Your egg will no longer be pretty and round, but should shrivel and turn brown. This is a great experiment to do with your kids, to explain to them what happens to our cells when we consume sugar.

Ocean in a Bottle

Every year we make a trek to the Outer Banks of North Carolina. We love to watch the waves crash against the sandy beaches. This simple science experiment is inspired by our weeks at the sea.

A wave transfers energy, not water. The water stays in the same place and passes kinetic energy. This wave in a bottle is fun to make and has the bonus that the finished product is mesmerizing to watch. In addition to being a great way to learn about waves and tides, the ocean bottle is a nice calm-down bedtime or naptime activity.

Materials

+ NONMETALLIC GLITTER (OPTIONAL)
+ EMPTY, CLEAN PLASTIC BOTTLE, WITH A SECURE TOP
+ HANDFUL OF SMALL SHELLS
+ BLUE FOOD COLORING
+ ENOUGH BABY OIL TO FILL THE PLASTIC BOTTLE HALFWAY
+ GLUE

TIP

This is a great time-out activity. Ask your child to sit calmly and watch the waves settle after the bottle has been shaken. Your child can get up once the sand glitter is back on the bottom of the bottle.

Pour ½ inch (1.3 cm) or so of plastic glitter crystals into the bottom of your bottle. It is best to use glitter that is not metallic. The metal-based glitters tend to corrode in water after a while. Add a couple of shells. Fill your bottle halfway with blue water. Top off the bottle with the baby oil. Be sure to leave about an inch (2.5 cm) of "air space" at the top.

Glue the bottle top securely to the bottle to avoid spills.

Shake the bottle to explore how waves are formed.

How does the earth's tilt affect the waves of the ocean?

Tilt the bottle onto its side and slightly shift the bottle to simulate the earth's rotation on its axis. Watch what happens to the waves. This shift of the water is similar to the tidal waves that our oceans experience as the earth rotates and tilts around the moon and the sun, as the gravitational pull moves the waters of the ocean.

What happens when the bottom of the ocean floor shifts? Bang the bottle. Can you see the water fluctuate?

Modifications for Younger Kids

Use the bottle as a vacation reminder. Let younger kids help decide what to put in the bottle. Start with sand and some shells collected at the beach. Add a little silver glitter, but keep it quietly ocean-like. It is a sweet thing to keep out to trigger vacation memories.

Modifications for Older Kids

In addition to using glitter and creating an ocean bottle—grab another water bottle and do an experiment, testing the dirt in your backyard. Grab a couple of cups of soil from your backyard. Fill your bottle with the soil, leaving an inch (2.5 cm) or two of space. Fill the bottle with water. Shake. Watch the sediment layers of the different components of your soil form.

Sandbox Volcano

My boys have been obsessed with volcanoes. On family road trips we often drive by an extinct volcano that sits close to the highway. It towers above the otherwise flat land and is the only landmark for miles and miles. Each time we pass it there is a heated discussion about what would happen if it erupted as we passed and suspicion that it really isn't extinct.

This harmless volcano can be made in the kids' sandbox next to toy car highways to experiment with the "what if" of kids' minds. You may not have magma handy, but since you hold the vinegar and baking soda, you determine when the volcano erupts!

Materials

+ Funnel
+ Empty plastic water bottle with a secure top
+ Baking soda
+ Squirt of whipping cream
+ Red food coloring
+ Sandbox (backyard dirt works great, too)
+ Vinegar

TIP

This could be done in the kitchen sink or bathtub, with a volcano mountain made out of tinfoil.

Using a funnel, fill the water bottle halfway with baking soda. Then add a little bit of whipping cream. On top of that, add the food coloring.

Put the top on the water bottle. Take the bottle filled with goo out to the sandbox and bury it so just the neck of the bottle is exposed.

Once the volcano has been fully constructed, take the cap off the water bottle and pour in the vinegar.

Watch the lava flow down the mountain and redirect any toy traffic that may be headed for doom.

Modifications for Younger Kids

Adults or older kids can create what is inside the water bottle and younger kids can construct what is outside.

Modifications for Older Kids

The addition of whipping cream makes the eruption less violent and thicker. Older kids can experiment with various degrees of lava thickness for the perfect natural disaster.

Snack Map

I was pretty sure someday I would happen across a treasure map. It would be on faded, crinkled parchment with old ink faded due to age. In one corner would be a big X that marked the spot of the treasure I would dig up. Likely, pirates would have abandoned the search, but I am very persistent and would find the chest of gold. It hasn't happened . . . yet.

This activity uses snack time as an excuse to have a fun treasure hunt around the house. It helps kids learn map reading skills and is sure to become a family favorite.

Materials
+ PAPER—ONE PAGE PER MAP
+ MARKERS
+ STICKER DOTS (OPTIONAL)
+ SNACKS IN PLASTIC CUPS OR WRAPPERS TO BE HIDDEN

Create a basic floor plan sketch of your home, adding in a few details here and there to define the space, such as the stove, fireplace, couch, door and bookshelves.

Use sticker dots to mark where the snacks are located if you want to be able to reuse the map, or mark with an X for onetime use.

Leave the snack map in a place where the kids will find it, then stand back and watch the fun.

Modifications for Younger Kids
Draw a picture of just one room and help them identify the landmarks on the map.

Laminate the map so kids can hide toys for one another and then reuse the map, marking the toy's hidden location.

Modifications for Older Kids
Make the map more complicated or just give them directions based on landmarks, left/right or compass directions.

Bath Sparkling Stones

Kids tend to have a good connection with rocks because they are easy to collect. We took the rock inspiration a bit further and creating bathtub "sparkly stones."

The basis of this recipe is Epsom salt, which isn't really a salt. It is a naturally occurring mineral called magnesium sulfate. Not only can it help you get clean, but it also has relaxation properties. This recipe can be modified to customize the scent, which just may encourage longer baths and cleaner results!

Materials
(to make about eight sparkling stones)

+ 1 CUP (240 G) EPSOM SALT
+ FOOD COLORING
+ 1 TABLESPOON (14 G) BAKING SODA
+ 1 ½ TABLESPOONS (22 ML) LEMON JUICE (USE PLAIN WATER IF YOU DO NOT WANT THE ROCKS TO FIZZ)
+ PLASTIC CUPS/BOWLS
+ ABOUT 8 SMALL DISPOSABLE CUPS, SUCH AS DIXIE
+ PLASTIC SPOON OR STIRRING STICK
+ ESSENTIAL OILS FOR SCENT (OPTIONAL)

Mix the Epsom salt, 4 drops of food coloring, baking soda and lemon juice together in an oversize plastic cup or bowl. Add a drop or two of essential oil to create the desired scent.

Repeat for additional colors and scents.

To make salt rocks, press the mixture into the bottom of a disposable cup about 2 inches (5 cm) deep. If you want a variety of colors, layer the colors in a plastic display container using the back of a spoon or a stirring stick to push each layer down. Set aside overnight to dry. Gently press out from the bottom of the cup to retrieve the final bath salt stone. Add the rock to your next bath.

Seal and store next to the tub for decoration or bath use.

Modifications for Younger Kids
Create the recipe, leaving out the essential oils. Also, be sure to watch that your children don't eat the salt—Epsom salt is inedible. You can replace the salt with baking soda alone. The rocks won't be as pretty but will be harmless if ingested.

Modifications for Older Kids
Add another layer of complication to your science experiment. Try to create fizzling stones. It took my elementary-school-age kids a couple of tries, but they had a blast mixing ingredients until they discovered a mixture that fizzled. They doubled the baking soda in the rock (as the chemical base) and added vitamin C powder (for the acid).

And then this is the tricky part . . . you will want to put in just enough liquid to be able to press the minerals together and form a stone, but be careful. If you put in too much, the stone will start fizzing before it is finished. Using very little water, press the ingredients into your mold and let it dry. To activate the "fizz," drop the stone into water. Your sparkly stone will now bubble.

Germs, Germs, Germs

While germs may be perceived as bugs, the truth is that we can't see them without a microscope. There are many types of germs, including bacteria, viruses, fungi and protozoa. They are miniature invaders that can be warded off by a serious hand-washing attack!

It can be challenging for kids to get the concept of fully washing their hands when they *look clean*. It is easier to quickly wash by running hands under water with little or no soap.

This activity can tangibly show the importance of hand washing and how germs can be places even when you can't see them.

Materials
+ SPRAY BOTTLE
+ 3 SLICES OF BREAD
+ 3 RESEALABLE PLASTIC SANDWICH BAGS
+ MARKER TO LABEL THE BAGS

TIP
Cover kids' hands with fine glitter and then use a flashlight to watch how it transfers when things are touched. Then have them try to wash the glitter off their hands completely.

Lightly spray the three slices of bread with water.

Have an older child or adult wash his/her hands thoroughly and then place one piece of bread into a bag, seal it and label it #1.

For bag #2, let kids handle the bread without washing their hands and then seal it.

With the third piece of bread, let the kids rub it between their hands, along the kitchen counter, and even drop it on the floor. Seal it into the remaining bag and label it #3.

Leave the baggies in a dark space for a couple of days.

Make a simple table with predictions from each child as to what each piece of bread will look like in a few days.

In our most recent experiment, bag #1 hadn't changed much. Bag #2 had some interesting white and crusty yellow growth on it. But the one that was the most colorful was the third piece of bread. It had significant growth of some funky green fuzzy stuff.

Modifications for Younger Kids
Use pictures to label the bags and table so they can remember which bag contains the bread that went through each process.

Modifications for Older Kids
Older kids can create a larger experiment by exposing bread slices to specific household surfaces and then charting the results.

Number Detective

Kids love a good mystery. In a book, the clues unravel page by page until the case is solved. In a movie, each scene intertwines information necessary to figure out the solution.

You won't need a magnifying glass or a tweed cap for this mystery, but you will need to raid your recycling bin and get ready for some number fun.

- -

Materials
+ 10 EMPTY WATER BOTTLES
+ PAINT—A LEFTOVER GALLON (4 L CAN) OF PAINT WORKS BEST
+ CARDBOARD
+ 10 SHARPENED PENCILS
+ 55 MARBLES

TIP
When you are done with your bottles, prop them open and play a game of bowling. Roll a ball at the bottle pins and see how many you can knock down.

Create a series of ten identical containers out of empty water bottles. Dip each water bottle into old paint and then turn upside down to dry. I used a homemade drying rack made of a piece of folded cardboard punctured by ten sharpened pencils, allowing the bottles to stay secure on the pencil base.

Once dried, distribute the marbles into the ten containers. Put one marble in the first bottle, two marbles in the second bottle, three marbles in the third bottle and so on. Fill all the bottles, ending with the tenth bottle having ten marbles.

You could use any containers you have around the house, or if you don't feel like painting, covering the bottles with construction paper could work well, too.

The object is to let kids put the bottles in order from one marble inside to ten marbles inside by using their detective skills: How heavy is the bottle? How many marbles does it sound as if there are inside when you shake the bottle? How does that compare to the bottle you just evaluated?

Modifications for Younger Kids
Pick out two or three of the bottles that have a wide difference in the number of marbles inside, like one, five and ten.

If they identified the order correctly, then hand them another bottle to see whether they can figure out where it might fit.

Modifications for Older Kids
Remove two of the bottles and mix them up again. Have the player try to guess which numbers were removed.

Pneumatic Motor

Air is a funny thing. It is everywhere, but we can't really see it. We know it is there when it moves, smells funny or changes temperature.

Air pressure is the push air places on everything. Since air molecules are far apart, they can be compressed to fit into a smaller space. A pneumatic device uses the expansion of the air for work.

This pneumatic motor uses a homemade version of bellows. With a push, it can create a flow of air behind a object. Even though you can't see the air, you will see the results.

Materials
+ 2 KITCHEN SPONGES
+ RESEALABLE PLASTIC BAG
+ DRINKING STRAW
+ TAPE
+ SMALL LIGHT TOYS
  (E.G., POM-POM, SMALL BALL,
  TOY CAR, HAIR BOW, ETC.)

TIP
Make two of these and play a game of table-top air soccer with makeshift goals at each end of the playing field.

Place two kitchen sponges, one on top of the other, inside the plastic bag.

Insert a drinking straw between the two sponges so that one end of the straw is inside the bag and the other end is sitting outside the bag.

Seal the bag and then secure it with tape.

Place a pom-pom on a flat surface and place the bag behind it so that the straw is positioned to blow the pom-pom. Press down hard on the sponges and watch the pom-pom roll away!

To get a stronger pump of air, blow into the straw, filling up the bag, and then repeat the process.

Modifications for Younger Kids
Instead of adding sponges and a straw to push items, simplify the experiment. Just fill a resealable plastic bag with air, seal it shut, then "pop" it open by pushing on the top of the bag (or even jumping on it). Your kids will be surprised with a bang! When air pressure changes quickly it creates a bang—much like the thunder in a storm.

Modifications for Older Kids
Have older kids hold the bag at different angles and propel objects of different sizes and weights.

Spiderweb Door

Spiderwebs are fascinating and beautiful. My mom and I used to hunt for the biggest and most complicated spiderwebs. The best time to find them is early in the morning while the dew is still fresh, making the webs glisten in the light.

This spiderweb inspired activity is perfect for a rainy day stuck indoors. Getting kids active in limited space is one of the challenges of parenthood. Time to spin our own web!

Negotiating passage through the spider web will stress kids' balance and challenge their kinesthetic awareness. Repeated practice will help them become more coordinated and improve proprioception (a sense of where your body is in space/relation to itself).

Materials

+ PAINTER'S TAPE
+ BALL OF YARN
+ BALLOON OR LIGHTWEIGHT BALL

TIP

Want to recreate a spider web that mimics the silk's stickiness? Substitute tape for the yarn in this activity. It can be used for climbing or for catching thrown paper-wad "bugs."

Tape the yarn to the door in varying intervals to make a "web." You can experiment with which shapes and angles work best for the space and participants.

Kids can take turns climbing through the web. A balloon or light ball to toss back and forth will get kids problem solving in a coordinated effort.

Modifications for Younger Kids

Create a floor option for movement through the web for younger participants. It can still appear small and difficult, but taking out the necessity to move over an obstacle will make it easier.

Modifications for Older Kids

Have them try to get through the web without the yarn falling down. If that is not enough of a challenge, have them attempt to get through without even touching the yarn. They can work on setting up a new web with a completely different experience.

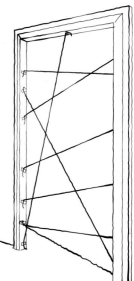

Tin Can Birdhouse and Feeder

Grandmother was a bird-watcher and would take her binoculars everywhere we walked. It was rare that she came across a bird that she didn't recognize and had to look up in her giant bird book.

This craft transforms a coffee can into a birdhouse and feeder. Situate this outside a window to bring bird life closer and observe the fun.

Materials
(to make one bird feeder)

+ CAN OPENER
+ LARGE COFFEE CAN WITH A LID
+ HEAVY-DUTY TAPE
+ THICK CARDBOARD
+ SCISSORS
+ BIRDSEED
+ HOLE PUNCH
+ SCREW
+ PENCIL
+ BITS OF YARN (OPTIONAL)
+ ROPE

Use a can opener to cut half of the bottom of the can. Have an adult carefully fold the half of the bottom in, forming a crescent. Be careful; the edges are sharp. Cover any remaining edges with heavy tape. Cut a circle from the cardboard to fit into the center of the can. Use tape to secure the circle in the can. That circle becomes a divider for the two rooms in the can. On the side with the half-circle, fill the bottom with birdseed.

Cut a circle opening in the lid of the coffee can. With a hole punch, make a hole below the large circle. Stuff a pencil into that hole. Secure the lid to the can with heavy-duty tape. The pencil is the perch. You can fill the house section with some bits of yarn to make it appealing for nest building.

We collected twigs from around our yard, which were secured to the sides with a glue gun.

Screw a hole in the side of the can and use yarn to hang it. Try to hang the can away from tree limbs and the house will help maintain it as a bird vs. squirrel house.

Modifications for Younger Kids
Younger kids can decorate the can lid for a special bird "front door."

Modifications for Older Kids
Older kids can design birdhouse/feeder decor. The decoration options are limitless and could coordinate with whatever they dream up.

Musical Science Pool

While banging merrily away, and without realizing it, your children are learning about sound waves and how beats "feel" in addition to the sound they hear. They are exploring the different reactions that applied force cause on the pan.

The vibrations created through banging can be manipulated with various water levels, resulting in a different pitch. Pitch is what our eardrum interprets from sound vibrations. This activity may sound like complete chaos, but a kiddie pool is the perfect laboratory for discovery!

Materials

+ Kiddie pool or shallow area of a larger pool
+ A collection of metal pots and pans
+ Metal spoons
+ Tin cans in a variety of sizes and shapes (with any sharp edges filed down)

Situate the kids in the water where they can be seated comfortably.

Turn a pot upside down just above water level. Bang on the pot with a spoon while you lower it into the water. Notice that the pitch of the drum changes as the water level rises in the pot.

Explore the strength of water's surface tension. As you fill a pot, turn it upside down in the pool (trying to keep the water inside), and pull the pot up. If you are careful, you can see the water lift as you pull the pot up.

You can also fill the cans with water. Tap the sides of the cans. Explore the sounds coming from the cans. How does the sound change as you pour more water into the can?

Put a small water puddle on the top of a drum. Bang the drum sides gently. What happens to the water on the top of the drum? Can you see the sound waves in the water puddle?

Modifications for Younger Kids
After making noise with the pots and pans, your child will probably enjoy simply pouring the water from container to container. This makes a good bath activity as long as the noise/mess isn't going to be an issue!

Modifications for Older Kids
Use various levels of water in a collection of cups to create a scale. Try to play a tune.

Acknowledgments

Many thanks to Page Street Publishing Company for making this book possible. A big thanks to Tamara Lee-Sang for the gorgeous photography. Much appreciation to Cathi & Kein Walsh, Cole Kaemmerling, Chanda & Audrey Schuh, the Knutson Kids, the Jones Boys, the McCullough Crew and Rhys Kiester for loaning their faces and passion for play to our book. May extra patience be awarded as gratitude to Carly Kaemmerling, Jana & Andrea Stout, Mary Ann Homer and Brent Moore for assistance with the photo sessions. We are grateful to Fred & Virginia Harder for inviting us into their amazing backyard.

Extra hugs to our nine collective children who are subjected to activity experiments on a regular basis while being photographed.

Inspirational Resources

In no particular order, we want to acknowledge our heartfelt gratitude to these bloggers and authors who have inspired and supported us as we have created this book.

We love them and think you will, too!

Shauna Callaghan—ShaunaCallaghan.com

Havalyn Nauss—Little Right Leg

Andie Jaye Cord—Crayon Freckles

Laurie Turk—Tip Junkie

Amy Locurto—Living Locurto

Rebecca Darling—R We There Yet Mom?

Catherine Toner—Nurture Store

Jamie Fink—Soph and Lulu

Joel Henriques—Made by Joel

Kristina Buskirk—Toddler Approved

Sarah Dees—Frugal Fun for Boys

Jennifer Haas—Plain Vanilla Mom

Katey Magill—Having Fun at Home

Trisha Stanley—Inspiration Laboratories

Zina Harrington—Let's Lasso the Moon

Rachelle Doorley—Tinkerlab

Amanda Morgan—Not Just Cute

Chrissy Watson—The Outlaw Mom

Jean Van'tHul—Artful Parent

Deborah Stewart—Teach Preschool

Jeanette Nyberg—Artchoo

Stacy Teet—Kid Stuff World

Pauline Soo—Lessons Learnt Journal

Jamie Reimer—Hands on: As We Grow

Asia Citro—Fun at Home with Kids

Mary-Ann Widhalm—Counting Coconuts

Kim Chance—Savor the Days

Ness Hoffman—One Perfect Day Blog

Donna Ridley-Burns—PlayBasedLearning.com

Anna Ranson—The Imagination Tree

Stephanie Morgan—Modern Parents Messy Kids

Marnie Craycroft—Carrots Are Orange

Elise & Emma—A Beautiful Mess

Deidre Smith—Jdaniel4's Mom

Amy—Stuck Under a Baby

Mari Hernandez—Inspired by Family

Liz Neiman—Love and Marriage Blog

Valerie Deneen—Inner Child Fun

Melissa Taylor—Imagination Soup

Jillian Riley—A Mom with a Lesson Play

Allison McDonald—No Time for Flash Cards

Tiffany Dahle—Peanut Blossom

Alissa Marquess—Creative with Kids

Mariah Bruehl—Playful Learning

Maggie Woodley—Red Ted Art

Megan Sheakoski—Coffee Cups and Crayons

Heather Williams, Erin Folkerts & Katherine Boyer

Index

About the Authors

Holly Homer is a "retired" physical therapist. Her kinesiology knowledge is put to the test daily while she tries to wear out her three boys. She adores that there is never a dull moment in her home even though it means the dining room table is never clear of kid projects.

Rachel Miller has been educating children for more than 15 years, in a variety of settings. As mom to six of the silliest kids in the universe, she enjoys discovering moments to explore and enjoy the world with her family. When she isn't finger painting, collecting bugs or doing laundry, you can find her writing